CO DURHAM

Edited by Michelle Warrington

First published in Great Britain in 1999 by
POETRY NOW YOUNG WRITERS
Remus House
Coltsfoot Drive, Woodston,
Peterborough, PE2 9JX
Telephone (01733) 890066

HB ISBN 0 75430 379 9
SB ISBN 0 75430 380 2

FOREWORD

This year, the Poetry Now Young Writers' Kaleidoscope competition proudly presents the best poetic contributions from over 32,000 up-and-coming writers nationwide.

Successful in continuing our aim of promoting writing and creativity in children, each regional anthology displays the inventive and original writing talents of 11-18 year old poets. Imaginative, thoughtful, often humorous, *Kaleidoscope Co Durham* provides a captivating insight into the issues and opinions important to today's young generation.

The task of editing inevitably proved challenging, but was nevertheless enjoyable thanks to the quality of entries received. The thought, effort and hard work put into each poem impressed and inspired us all. We hope you are as pleased as we are with the final result and that you continue to enjoy *Kaleidoscope Co Durham* for years to come.

CONTENTS

Fyndoune Community College

Laura Sutton	73
Diane Boyd	73
Helen Pinkney	74
Leanne Bromley	74
Melissa Sweeney	75
Vicky McLaughlin	75
Aimee Wilson	76
Victoria Bramble	76
Mark Nelles	77

Hurworth Comprehensive School

David Ellis	77
Peter Hedley	78
Amy Sedgwick	78
Heather Minto	79
Andrew Birbeck	80
Jennie Haines	80
Adam Wilkinson	81
Kayleigh Evans	82
Steven Wilson	83
Sarah McNulty	83
Sarah-Jane Brown	84
Emma Graham	84
Laura Louise Foers	85
Holly Avery	86
Laura Bernstone	86
Chris Harrison	87
Nichola Ingledew	87
Clare Blacklee	88
Gemma Harris	88
Laura Todd	89
Robert Lawrence	90
Toni Leach	90
Nicola Foster	91
Phillip Sievers	92
Kati Hayllar	92
Vickie Robinson	93

Nicola Fullard	94
Kelly Pybus	95
Gemma Roberts	95
Chris Devlin	96
Sarah Welch	97
Sean Lamb	97
Lauren Drysdale	98
Alex Minto	98
Pippa Baker	99
Philip Masters	100
Emma Samuels	100
Emma Todd	101
Victoria Chisholm	102
Anthony Scott	102

Hurworth House School

Christopher Hedley	103
James Gale	103
Martin Nichols	104
Richard Phillips	104
Jonathan White	105
Miles Newton	105
Matthew Gale	105
Alex Strachan	106

Moorside Comprehensive School

Kris Suddick	106
Abbie Whitehead	107
Jessica Maughan	108
Gregg Allaker	108
Kirsty Grant	109
Kerry Mordue	110
Leanne Elliott	110
Kirstin McGuigan	111
Stephen Westgarth	112
Callie O'Brien	113
Kirsty Baum	114
Jemma Green	114

The Poems

A PART OF WAR

The large monstrous beast moved along the grey charred battlefield.
Under its own power it conquered hills and obstacles
of dead corpses - which were once fighting men.
A few dirty exhausted soldiers in old torn uniforms
wearily trotted behind the beast for cover
from the biting machine-gun fire.
A large mist shielded their position from the enemy mortar
which exploded and tore up the dead ground.
The seemingly endless mist and mortar fire
soon encouraged the men to move from their cover
into the white mist . . .
They went - *never to be seen again!*
Christopher Massey (15)
Carmel RC School

AUTUMN

As I stand staring out of the window
watching the autumnal world below,
I see the leaves drift from the trees
and crawl along the frosty earth
like an evil omen bringing the cold.
A sea of yellows
golds
browns and deep reds
dance before my eyes.
It's autumn.
We wait for the chill
that lies ahead.
Francesca Denham (13)
Carmel RC School

AUTUMN

Summer is gone, autumn is here
and winter seems so very near,
with the cold and nipping frost,
the fun and playtimes seem to be lost.
Sad little faces peer through the windowpane,
but all that they see is the splashing of the rain.
No sun can be found, not one ray!
Even though the children pray and pray.
The rain has stopped but the wind does roar,
the leaves are falling, more and more.
Leaves are swirling to the ground,
conkers are lying all around.
They realise that you don't need sun
to have a laugh and some fun!
Running outside with coats zipped up to the top,
they run, they jump, they skip and they hop
through leaves that crackle under their feet,
they rub their hands together for a little bit of heat.
It's getting colder every day.
Hello winter! Come and stay!

Hannah Davies (12)
Carmel RC School

A CHILDREN'S MOON

Moon, why are you in the sky?
The night is gone, the day is nigh.
Now's the time to see the sun.
We'll see you when the day is done.

Moon, go back to your bed.
Rest your tired sleepy head.
Now's the morning not the night.
Later, you can spread your light.

Clare McGuckin (14)
Carmel RC School

CHANGE . . .

A mass of leaves lay softly on the ground
Until the breeze came to swirl them around
And make the huge trees roar
Whilst I looked on in awe!
Soon the breeze turned into rain
The frost is here and snow is lain.
Night falls in the blink of an eye
Leaving an icy winter's sky.
But just as the greyness set in
A miracle starts to begin.
Surprises begin to uncoil
As a new lease of life comes from the soil.
The spring was a nice retreat
But the summer brought on the heat.
As I lay in the sun and the haze
I suddenly realised it was all a phase,
Because over the field came a breeze
Which caused havoc with the trees
And as I listened to the rushing sound
I realised what goes around - comes around . . .
Emma Whitfield (14)
Carmel RC School

A POEM ABOUT PIGEONS

Pigeons are beggars - roaming the streets,
Eating any food their small eyes meet.
They raid you in parks and attack you in your tracks.
The pigeons drop bombs and stain your new anoraks.

They attack other birds and peck at your head,
Pigeons are nasty and steal all your bread.
They wait under park benches - waiting for a crumb,
If they can't find anything they peck at your bum!

You can see them soar high in the sky,
Never knowing to where they will fly.
They sleep on very high buildings at night,
They often blend in and stay out of sight.

They stay inactive on many monuments,
Pigeons sometimes look like little ornaments.
Some wear tags on their small pink feet,
Most fly about in a big fleet.

Many pigeons are shot from the skies
There are so many - nobody cries.
After all, we will never know
Where do all the dead pigeons go!

Adam Ayre-Garcia (14)
Carmel RC School

AUTUMN HAS COME

In Britain long ago red crusty leaves falling
out of trees, plants dying every day.

People walking through the leaves,
crunch, crunch as they walk.

Berries and conkers falling down,
children searching for those conkers,
squirrels look for their food for winter has come.

Old people brushing the leaves away
and blossom is no more.

William Barras (11)
Carmel RC School

FOUR SEASONS

Spring, summer, autumn and winter
Four contrasting seasons throughout the year.
It starts with winter.
Flakes falling and wind blowing,
Children playing in the snow.
Curling up by the fire with a rosy glow.
Time moves on, the seasons change.
By March the sun is starting to shine,
The birds are singing and the air is warm.
Spring glides into summer,
The finest season of them all.
Blue skies and blazing heavens.
It's the time of the year for bathing in the sun.
The summer is cruelly short-lived.
Before you know it, the leaves are cascading from their trees.
Autumn is the first sign that winter is on its way.
The seasonal colours changing from a luscious green of summer
to a murky brown of autumn.
Sadly it's that time of the year again when the wind is whistling.
To see the sun is a rarity,
Soon enough the seasonal circle is back to its source.
The chilling wind piercing your skin -
as the snow makes its home on the Earth's surface.

Michael Megowan (14)
Carmel RC School

THE STORM

The nights were getting darker, the sun was going down.
The wind was getting fiercer, the howling grew in sound.
The trees were bare - the plants were dead
The animals had all gone to bed.
The winter snow was thick and deep
Children in their beds were fast asleep,
When all of a sudden the wind broke loose
And went through the land with a terrible whoosh!
Branches were felled, power lines brought down
Tiles ripped off - thrown to the ground.
At morning dawn, children looked out
To see the destruction caused
While the lights were out . . .

Helen McAninly (14)
Carmel RC School

AUTUMN

Cold frosty mornings,
Jack Frost is here,
Time for hats and gloves again,
And sitting round the fire.

Carpets of leaves, autumn fruits,
Shiny green conker cases,
A blaze of red, orange and russet,
As the leaves swirl around me.

A season of festivals,
A celebration of harvests and gunpowder plots,
Children with their lanterns and masks,
Penny for the guy, trick or treat.

Joanna Reed (12)
Carmel RC School

KALEIDOSCOPE

Each morning in a blustery run,
the leaves alight in the dusky sun.
Catching in the droplets of the morning dew,
a kaleidoscope of radiant purples and blue.
In my desperate sprinting rush
I catch a glimpse of my bus.
I tear myself away from this magnificent view,
knowing that each day that comes will bring
something new . . .
A week goes by and the leaves are rotten,
decayed and old the spectacular displays forgotten.
Finally the sky fades to blacks and greys,
stormy and drizzly changing days.
Season going to icy and cold
Dark and stormy - Christmas tales start to be told!
Weather's different - nothing will grow
One week later I awake to a cover of
snow . . . !

Danielle Miller (15)
Carmel RC School

AUTUMN

Autumn is here, the leaves are falling,
People still in bed snoring and snoring.
Robins and squirrels, gathering food,
And hedgehogs hibernating, waiting and waiting till the end.
People lighting fires, bonfires and fireworks,
getting dressed up for All Hallows Eve.
Children collecting conkers from the nearby trees.
Lakes and rivers freezing over.
People feeding animals so they don't die of hunger.

Thomas Brockley (11)
Carmel RC School

AUTUMN

Outside it seems so cold, so lonely
because nobody's around.
When you look out of your window
all you can see are golden brown leaves.
Twirling, twirling to the ground
All the leaves have fallen off the trees
We know it's not summer
because there's hardly any bees.
All we want to do is go inside
where it's nice and warm
rather than outside
facing a cold storm!
Laura Elliott (14)
Carmel RC School

AUTUMN

Orange, copper, red and gold
The weather's starting to get cold
Conkers falling from their tree
Children gather them happily
The days get shorter, the nights grow long
The birds wake early to sing their song
Autumn's almost over, winter's near
Before I know it Christmas'll be here.
Josie Miller (12)
Carmel RC School

SAME OLD MONDAY MORNING . . .

'Ten past seven - time to wake up!'
Calls the infamous voice outside my door.
Weekend's gone - time to go back to school.
What an absolute bore!

Outside of my window, puddles were forming,
The crystal-like raindrops bouncing off the ground.
The rain and wind lashing against the windows,
The atmosphere grey and dim all around!

Time for the same old routine,
Brush my teeth and get a wash.
Get dressed into my school uniform.
Have a breakfast of toast and orange squash.

Drive to school in our school bus,
The kids at the front - immature as ever!
Arrive at school and straight to Registration.
The noise in the class leaves the teacher at the end of her tether!

The first lesson - English!
Our work is on a book about witches,
Outside the window it's still raining heavier than ever
Because all you can see is waterlogged pitches.

English is over and now it's break
Second lesson - chemistry has us yawning,
Only 20 minutes to go then lunch,
Next week it will be exactly the same thing
Same old Monday morning . . . !

Becki Smith (14)
Carmel RC School

NO IDEAS . . .

I'm sitting here trying to write,
A poem that's nice and bright.
No ideas, nothing at all,
It's driving me up the wall . . .
I'm waiting for an inspiring thought,
But nothing so far, I'm up to nought.
I'd do anything to get some ideas
To do with laughter - or with tears.
I still haven't got a good subject
So there isn't any poem yet!
When I've found something to do,
I'll write it down and give it to you.
I might get a theme, sometime today,
Until then, there is nothing to say.
I need some ideas to enter my brain,
Just to stop me going insane.
I've just realised what I've done
Rushed ahead, jumped the gun
Before I've managed to think of anything
Here is written - my attempted poem!
Paul Trenholme (14)
Carmel RC School

THE MOON . . . THE MOON

The moon, the moon
far up there?
Looking down
with a stare!
Sometimes dull
sometimes bright
Yet you're always
giving light!
When I look
up from planet earth.
I often wonder
how old, far and
great you are!
You have so much
power over us with
tides as we ride
through outer space.
So ending this
I think of you
wishing, wondering
what's it like to be you!
Martyn Pease (14)
Carmel RC School

MY FIRST DAY AT CARMEL

The alarm clock woke me up,
at half-past seven.
I went to get a wash,
as slow as I could,
I got dressed then had breakfast,
but I could hardly eat,
I was like a bag of nerves,
it was time to go.
I walked into school,
I saw Lee - a friend of mine,
we walked side by side.
To start an important journey in our lives.
We went to the front doors,
we lined up in our forms,
then when everybody arrived, we entered the hall.
We sat in our forms,
and we had an assembly,
then we went to our form rooms.
We were given diaries,
and a lesson schedule,
then started our first lessons at Carmel.
First we had music,
it was very hard!
Then it was science,
it was very boring.
Then the moment I'd been waiting for
Ring! Ring! Ring!
It was the end of my first day at Carmel . . .

James Parkinson (15)
Carmel RC School

IN THE AUTUMN

In the autumn all the leaves fall off the trees,
And cover the land with a blanket of red, orange, gold and brown.
In the autumn the leaves swirl in a misty breeze,
And heather covers the moors in a purple crown.

In the autumn Jack Frost leaves a shiny glistening trail upon the ground,
And the orange glow of a bonfire lights up the sky.
In the autumn the birds migrate without a sound,
And the colours of the flowers fade and die.

In the autumn the hedgehogs snuggle together in amongst the leaves,
And the red-breasted robin brightens up the dull days.
In the autumn a swirl of icy wind travels across the seas,
And the world can be seen through a foggy haze.

In the autumn!
Katrina Busby (12)
Carmel RC School

WHY?

I have never understood why people pick on me,
just because of the way I look.
The verbal abuse never stops.
Someone always looks at me and makes a
spiteful comment, under their breath.
As I climb off the bus, they spit on me
and tell me to go back to where I belong.
I have no trust,
I have no friends,
I have no self-confidence,
and I have no way of expressing my feelings.
All because my skin is black.

Linsey Stevens (14)
Carmel RC School

AUTUMN

The crisp autumn leaves fall gently to the ground,
A blizzard of colours,
Russet, bronze, auburn, golden browns, yellows, greens,
Conkers and acorns cluster in the trees,
Bright red berries lie mottled in the bushes.

Jack Frost comes creeping up,
Shiny, sparkling ice spreads across the windowpanes,
Plants begin to droop and blossom is no more,
The sun hangs low in the sky and nights darken.

Bangers, rockets and Catherine wheels shoot sparks
of bright colours up into the sky,
Little witches, goblins and devils come knocking on doors,
Farmers gather in their harvest,
Animals snuggle down into their comfy beds
and robins fly in and cosy in the haylofts.

Saskia Van Vlijmen (11)
Carmel RC School

MY FIRST DAY AT SCHOOL

I was nervous when I first started school
And wearing my uniform made me feel like a fool
I didn't know any of the different places
And I only knew a few people's faces
But now I'm getting to know people better
And now I've got to write my last teacher a letter
So I'm glad that I've started my secondary school
But in my blazer I still feel like a fool!

Sarah Flanagan (11)
Carmel RC School

IF THE WORLD WAS MADE OUT OF SWEETS

If the world was made out of sweets,
I'd eat it all day long.
My parents would say it's bad for me,
But it's so nice it can't be wrong.
When it rained, it would rain jelly babies
Falling from the sky.
I would simply stand there
With my mouth open wide.
When I work I'd write with chocolate ink,
The teachers would get in a rage,
Because every time I made a mistake,
I could just lick it off the page.
Smarties would grow on the tree tops,
There'd be an everlasting supply,
Only I would be able to reach them,
I'd make the other kids cry.
The only problem with my world
Is when the sun, it gleams,
Comes out and melts all of the chocolate
And shatters all my dreams.

Laura Wake (12)
Carmel RC School

AUTUMN

A utumn is coming with tasty blackberries
U pon the ground conkers start to fall
T he trees are bare, their branches all wiggly
U nder your feet the leaves are crisp and dry
M ornings are cold and misty when I wake up
N ight-times are dark and long, I can't play out.

Natasha Rogers (11)
Carmel RC School

HALLOWE'EN

In the blackness of the night,
Children shout and scream with fright.

Witches cackle and pumpkins laugh,
As people are drawn down the Devil's path.

Vampires bite and cauldrons bubble,
Give me a sweet or you're asking for trouble.

Flying bats, mummies' heads,
Monsters' blood and spiders' webs.

Trick or treat down the street,
Open the door or you're dead meat.

Knock knock at number eight,
Come out now before it's too late.

Come out now if you dare,
If you don't I'll give you a scare.

Step out now, you should be seen,
After all it's *Hallowe'en!*

Tom Stuart (12)
Carmel RC School

AUTUMN

A utumn is the season for getting ready for winter
U sing the scarves, carrots and more for the snowman
T eaching less and less but then no more
U sing the conkers on strings and playing games
M ore and more bare trees
N ow fireworks and shiny Jack Frost with mist in the sky.

Kelly Toole (11)
Carmel RC School

THE SEA

The sea is a never-ending story,
With countless stories to tell,
Ones of conquest,
Ones of adventure,
And some of sorrow too.
Masses of ships have sunk there,
With fortunes untold,
All hidden in the abyss below,
At the bottom of the deep blue sea.
On goes the battle between cliff and sea,
The sea is winning,
The ever-raging battle,
Biting chunks away from the cliff,
Leaves the cliff old and battered,
With not much to say.

Leon Watson (13)
Carmel RC School

MY GRAN

My gran was a leader to me,
my gran was a torch to me showing me right from wrong,
my gran was a carer for me, always there for me,
my gran was everything to me,
but now she's gone.

Marc Smith (12)
Carmel RC School

AUTUMN DAYS

I walk down the quiet street,
Either side of me I meet,
The tall dark trees, swaying in the breeze,
The golden on the leaves.

As I look up real high,
I see the misty clouds in the sky,
The sadness on the curling-up plants,
Lying on the ground amongst the little ants.

Then there's these lazy days,
Which give you the feeling of different ways,
The cold whispers in the winds,
The hidden animals living in bins.

I'd rather be in bed,
But I'm here instead,
All alone,
Wishing I was at home.

I'm feeling all weak,
And I'm still on this one street.

Sarah Christine Waring (11)
Carmel RC School

AUTUMN

Autumn is cold and bright,
Autumn has so many colours including red, gold and white.
Bonfires and fireworks brightly glow,
Animals in hibernation lost in the snow!

Rain, wind and snow,
Ice, leaves and bare trees.
Plants are dying, summer is lost,
Leave your house and frost!
Robin hiding in the tree until the wind takes the leaves,
Acorns and conkers fall from the trees.

Charlotte Oldham (11)
Carmel RC School

SEASONS

Winter is cold and the trees are bare,
haven't you got a bit of warmth to spare?
Snowballs thrown, snowman built,
this isn't the weather to wear a kilt.

Next onto spring with a mad March hare,
the trees among us are no longer bare.
Bees are buzzing round our heads,
we like to snuggle up in our beds.

Now we have summer, at last it's here,
people swimming in streams that look so clear.
Light warm nights,
we never need to switch on the lights.

Last we have autumn - leaves start to fall,
from green to brown they never call.
Fireworks bang, sparkle and fizz,
people going to parties think they look the biz.

They are the seasons,
we have them for many reasons.

Madelaine Haylett (12)
Carmel RC School

DARLO HC

Darlo HC, that's my team,
And they play just like a dream,
On my debut with Darlo,
We lost 5-0,
The next game we played,
We lost as well.

We practise on Tuesdays,
From half 6 till half 8,
And also on Fridays at school.
We practise our hitting,
And dribbling too,
And also we play a short game.

I'm proud to be from Darlo,
And play on their team,
Hockey's my game,
And hockey's my dream.

Andrew McKenzie (12)
Carmel RC School

THIS IS AUTUMN 1998

Autumn is the season of changing moods
Of warm colours - reds, golds and browns
Of cold frost and winter winds.

Autumn is the season of cool Hallowe'en nights
Of harvest corn and bare emptiness
It's woolly jumpers and frosty sunsets.

Autumn is the season of falling leaves
Of swirling mists and shiny berries
Of lively robins and hibernating animals.

Autumn is the season of children's conkers
Of thick coats and silent rain
Of sparkling fireworks cascading over dark pine cones.
Autumn is here!

Danielle Hossell (11)
Carmel RC School

WAR ZONE

The sound of bullets,
Crashing into the walls.
The sound of grenades,
Exploding in the trenches.
The noise was horrific,
Thud!
A man hit the ground.
I whipped a round of bullets
Into my gun,
One after one.
The explosions came closer, closer still.
The next one would surely kill me.
I began to run,
My feet hit hard against the dusty ground.
Thud, thud, thud, thud!
My mind was spinning,
I dived towards the underground shelter.
Phew! Safe at last,
For now.

Duncan Harrison (14)
Carmel RC School

PETS

Pets, pets, cute as can be,
they're part of the family.
Cats, dogs, hamsters and rabbits,
they all have dirty habits.
They don't clean up after themselves,
and they hide upon the shelves.
They wake you up during the night,
just when you are snuggled up tight.
They always want a lot of attention,
so when I'm late for school I get detention.
They need feeding, grooming and cleaning,
but they have a lot of meaning.

Andrea Hodgson (12)
Carmel RC School

AUTUMN

In the autumn stand the trees.
The wind blows and down fall the leaves.
There are different colours, red brown and yellow.
This is the time of year that makes you feel mellow.

Flowers don't grow.
Conkers falling to the leafy ground,
And Hallowe'en gives me a bit of a fright.
The nights get darker - no more light!

There are many different trees with no more leaves.
I don't want it to last forever.
And there is blossom no more.

Michael Baker (11)
Carmel RC School

AUTUMN IS . . .
Autumn is the crispy, golden leaves that float
to the ground.
They come from the bare, rustling trees,
that wave in the swirling winds.

Autumn is crackling bonfires, that look blinding
in the darkness of the night sky.
Fireworks that fly into space, bright colours drift
down from them.

Autumn is smoking chimneys, with frost sparkling
on the ground.
People with woolly jumpers, gloves and warm hats on.

Autumn is chirping robins that sing in the brown trees.
Animals are sneaking into their cosy beds for the winter.

'Blossom is no more!'
Ashleigh Stroud (12)
Carmel RC School

AUTUMN IS HERE
Discarded leaves fall from the trees old and dead they whisper silently.
Animals scurrying, collecting food among rusty piles of leaves.
As children hit the trees hoping for conkers to fall from the leaves,
More leaves tumble and alone they die, silent and each one rare, never
to be seen again.
The trees are dressed in yellows, oranges, golds and reds and soon the
grassy floor . . .
Autumn is here.
Katie Wray (12)
Carmel RC School

THE AUTUMN'S COMING TO AND THROUGH TIME FOR ME TO GO

The wind is howling in the mist
Soon I'll have to write my Christmas list
The twigs are broken on the ground
And the leaves are starting to make a mound
The crispy sounds of the leaves
Flying in the breeze
The autumn's coming to and through time for me to go.

The shiny colours on the floor
Make me want more and more
The animals starting their hibernation
A revolution driving through our glorious nation
Watching the birds flying high
Making me shout 'My o' my'
The autumn's coming to and through time for me to go.

Spring has gone, summer too
Hearing the cows go moo, moo, moo.
Now it's time for me to go
Getting ready for the snow
The autumn's coming to and through time for me to go.

John Clegg (13)
Carmel RC School

AUTUMN

Leaves start falling from the trees
There seem to be no more bees
Jumpers better come out soon
Hats, scarves, gloves too
Conkers start to fall
The children collect them all
If you have not noticed, *autumn* is here!

The night is long
The sun has gone
The summer birds start to go
They disappear into the foggy glow
The plants start to die because it's getting cold
The garden does not look so bold
If you have not noticed, *autumn* is here!

Natasha Whitfield (11)
Carmel RC School

THE DARK SEASON

The weather's changing,
The leaves are swirling, twirling to the ground,
The conkers smashing as they fall.

The colours are changing,
From light summer colours,
To warm golden autumn colours.

The edges of leaves are curling,
Making a crispy noise as people kick through the leaves,
They are changing from bright greens to golden browns.

The animals are going in for a long hibernation,
Dreading the long icy-cold season.

The fog, the mist and the bitter cold winds all rushing in,
With dull short days and dark long nights.

But then all clears up and the blossoms are out
Blooming once again.

Emilie-Louise Smith (13)
Carmel RC School

AUTUMN WAYS

Yes, it's come, autumn is here,
Nobody knows, but then we all cheer.
Tons and tons of golden-brown leaves,
Hardly any left on the trees.
Yes, yes, autumn is here.
The wind is here, gusty and bold,
I'm not going out, it's bound to be cold.
Round the window, this creature rattles,
Trying to get in this thing still battles.
Oh no, oh no, the big, bad-tempered wind is here!
Yes, yes, the leaves have come,
'Oh no,' cries my mum.
In I go; into the leaves,
Up and up, back up to the trees.
Yes, yes, autumn has arrived.
As I walk through the park,
I see leaves covered by bark.
The holey leaves no longer look nice,
They only look half-eaten by mice.
While green leaves turn to brown,
Then fall from branch to ground.
Animals prepare to sleep till spring,
Squirrels gathering nuts to homeward bring.
Hips and haws in autumn splendour,
Lead us into dark November.

This tatty place to me is unique,
People say it can be so bleak.
All I can see is a sea of golden-brown.

Listen . . .
I can't hear a single sound.
Clare Gale
Carmel RC School

AUTUMN
Golden leaves blow across the Dales,
It often rains and sometimes hails,
Shorter days and longer nights,
The moon is shining, silver and bright.

Wrapped up warm, you go out to play,
Red and gold leaves blow away,
Catch one and you make a wish,
But decide you are too selfish . . .

Hallowe'en comes, the ghouls surround you,
Some disguises completely astound you,
Children ask you 'Trick or treat?'
You decide to give them sweets.

Bonfire night gets nearer and nearer,
The stars at night get clearer and clearer,
Brilliant colours fill the sky,
As the fireworks start to fly.

Bare trees glisten on frosty mornings,
You realise winter is dawning,
Colder days and harsher nights,
Soon there will be snowball fights.

Eleanor Naseby (12)
Carmel RC School

MUSICAL VIBES

As loud music awakens me,
I look out the window and there I see,
An orchestra stomping out on the street,
I feel the vibrations of the noisy beats.

Bang, bang, on the drums,
The amplified sounds of the guitar strums,
The quiet strokes of the violin,
As the orchestra starts to come in.

I look closer to see the lovely parade,
As they walk down the street the music starts to fade,
The instruments and the sounds had all gone away,
And I no longer felt the vibes of the music that day.

Anne Marie Taberdo (12)
Carmel RC School

STREAM

The gushing stream,
Flows round the bend,
It sounds like a dream,
Never coming to an end.

Down the hill,
Jumping the stones,
Never being still,
It sounds like it moans.

The sea is drawing near,
The river is yet to be,
The roaring waves in your ear,
Now it's in the sea.

Emma Rowlinson (12)
Carmel RC School

DEEP SPACE

Up, up there in deep space,
An alien tries to wipe out the human race,
He thinks of killing us all with a single blow,
But he has a long way to go.

His ships are silver,
Ours are gold,
He is green and sneaky,
But we are brave and bold.

Zoom, zoom go the fighters,
Bang, bang go the guns,
Screams of pain and yells of joy,
But nobody wins,
Because war's a horrible thing.

Joe Weir (12)
Carmel RC School

THE BOMB BLAST

Running, racing, dashing to our shelter
Screaming, screeching, fills the air
And all I can see is darkness

We sit there silently, scared and unsure
Crying and cursing, commotion surrounds us
And all I can feel is darkness

Bombs crashing and booming nearby
A baby gives a silent cry
And all I can hear is darkness.

Claire McElvaney (13)
Carmel RC School

MY FIRST DAY AT CARMEL

As I stepped off the bus
My knees began to shake
I didn't know what to do
My teeth were chattering like an earthquake!

I looked so smart but felt so dumb
But then I thought this might be fun!

Carmel School is the best
Better than all the rest
I made new friends
The teachers are nice
It seems to me
I've made the right choice.

Emma Cawthorn (12)
Carmel RC School

DREAMS

D ark air around makes you fall asleep and dreary.
R eality hits fantasy in a mixed-up world.
E ternal images planted in your brain.
A gain and again strangers enter your head.
M ixed-up images, some good, some bad.
S trange, weird images dancing in your brain.

D ark rooms with white walls.
R ough surfaces which are smooth.
E verything is so mysterious.
A nimation being made in your brain.
M uffled voices, some screaming, some whispering.
S trange, virtual, so real are . . .
Dreams!
Emma Ovens (12)
Carmel RC School

MY FIRST DAY AT SCHOOL

It was my first day of school
I was nervous as could be
Seeing older, bigger people
Pushing and shoving around me.

We had an assembly
When we got into school
It was really weird
Obeying new rules.

The day didn't go by as fast as
I thought it would be
It was like I was in school for a whole century
But I enjoyed it there
It was OK
Although I didn't want to go there every day!

Clare Furlong (11)
Carmel RC School

WAR

Countryside a peaceful place
Until one day, disaster
A plane tried to bomb us to our death
Crashing and thudding all around us
Children running around crying
As homes are being destroyed
Trees around us are restless and
Rustling like bombs going off
Homes stood tall but then split into two parts
It's a war-torn junk yard.

Katie Tinkler (13)
Carmel RC School

SECONDARY SCHOOL!

Getting in the car at eight thirty-five,
Wondering what today will be like.
Will I enjoy it?
Will it be bad?
Or will it be just like any other day?
My mum pulled up to the big gates,
That lead the way to Carmel.
Standing at the door,
Waiting to go in,
I didn't know anybody there.
So many people looking at me,
Lost, lonely and frightened.
Into the hall,
We all sat down,
And said 'Good morning' to Miss Rotchell.
The day was going fine,
Yet I felt so small,
Against all the older people.
I wish I had gone to another school,
Like Haughton or Longfield,
But now I realise,
Carmel's the best,
Haughton and Longfield are history.

Natasha Toni Bree (11)
Carmel RC School

FEAR WITHIN ME

Fear ran down my spine,
the sound of agony, filled up my eyes.
Noises plummeted in the distance.
All around me people fell,
screaming and yelling in pain.

Overhead planes dropped their bombs,
people hurtled into shelters.
Mothers cried out for their loved ones.
Holes in the ground rumbled and thundered,
breaking up the ground.

As I watched people sprawled out around me,
and the groans of my friends,
one last bomb from above,
sent everyone flying, but me.

Rebecca Claire Allen (14)
Carmel RC School

SMILE!

The girl's mouth was pouted.
Someone told a joke.
Her lips parted showing a beautiful set of teeth
as white as snow, as straight as a ruler and
as clean as a new white plate.
Her lips spread out a mile and went up her cheeks to her eyes.
Her eyes sparkled like diamonds as blue as the sky on a clear day.
Her cheeks went pink with laughter like a clown's
and her nose scrunched up like a dog.
Her face lit up like a light bulb . . .

Catriona White (13)
Carmel RC School

THE CRISPY AUTUMN

Summer has ended, autumn's begun,
The crispy, crumply leaves have come.
They are falling, swirling to the ground,
They are so delicate, they don't make a sound.
The rough, knobbly conkers are bouncing to the floor,
The winds are howling with a mighty big roar.
The ground is a carpet of warm autumn colours,
People are playing out with their sisters and brothers.
The stiff, bent branches of the big bold trees,
Are swaying wildly in the gusty strong breeze.
Autumn is fading right into the past,
The Christmas trees and presents are here at last.

Susann McAllister (12)
Carmel RC School

WINTER SPEED

I am the winter, so fast and so cold
Blowing and blowing
Faster and faster.
I am the winter, so fast and so cold
Blowing away autumn
Faster and faster.
I am the winter, so fast and so cold
Blowing spring's hair
Faster and faster.
I am the winter now slow and old
Sleeping in spring beds
Slowing and stopping.

Christopher Byrne (11)
Carmel RC School

MY FIRST DAY AT SCHOOL

My first day at Carmel was scary,
I stood with a few friends from my primary school,
In front of the main doors.
I suddenly realised it had now begun,
A new day,
And a new school.
It was about five to nine when
Our head of year, Miss Rotchell came through.
She told us to line up in order of our forms.
The forms were 7C, 7A, 7R, 7E and 7L.
I was in 7C so I lined up in the first line.
We got lead in by our form tutor, Mr Madley,
He was new too.
I was nervous, suddenly my mind went blank,
I panicked, I didn't know my way round!
After assembly, we spent the whole morning with our form tutor,
And some of the afternoon.
I liked my form tutor.
Then once we finished our lesson with him,
We had English with Miss Gavaghan,
Where we started with a Blackwell spelling test.
Then all too soon the day was over,
And when I got home I collapsed
On my bed, completely exhausted.

Philip McLean (11)
Carmel RC School

IT HAS ARRIVED, HAVE YOU NOTICED?

Have you noticed it yet?
The winds are gusty and breezy.
The warm weather's gone,
It has finally arrived.

As you look out of your bedroom window,
What do you see? Trees with rusty coloured leaves,
And conker cases are dead and brown,
The shiny, polished conkers have gone.
The children have knocked them off the bare brown trees.

When you step outside, what do you hear?
Silence! Except the gusty, howling wind.
Animals are hibernating,
Birds have emigrated to warmer places.
The leaves are red and brown,
Crumpled, misshaped, frayed and dirty.

As you put on your winter coat,
You have finally realised that it is here.
Everything is dead and bare, leaves are falling,
Falling to the ground.
The trees are shedding their brown, rusty leaves.

As you walk down the leaf-covered path,
You start to hear little voices screaming and laughing.
As you get nearer and nearer the park, which was once so bright,
You find there is a sea of leaves and swaying little brown old trees.

Autumn has arrived.
Anna Robinson (13)
Carmel RC School

AN AUTUMN POEM

Autumn has come again,
Leaves falling,
Winds a'howling.
Yes, autumn is near.
Yes, autumn is here.

The sky is dull,
The rains fall.
Why is autumn such a miserable thing?
Conkers fall, falling, falling.
Leaves swirl, twirl, twisting, turning.

The trees are bare,
Their branches wear nothing but a bird's old nest.
The birds have gone.
The animals' preparation has been done.
The hibernating season has begun.

What is this I see?
A twinkle of early morning frost,
Covering the golden, red and auburn leaves
Which have already been tossed.

The sky is very dark grey.
The ground looks as if it's about to fray.
The last animal about to catch its prey.
Let the autumn change its way.

An old man warms by his bonfire,
Toasting a marshmallow on a wire.
I go and join him.
And from the sun it fades away.
Things become dim, so very dim.

Samantha Payne (12)
Carmel RC School

MY AUTUMN POEM

Autumn time has come around,
The dry crispy golden leaves fall to the ground,
There's a cold gentle breeze,
And all the trees have knobbly knees.

Conkers come shiny and polished,
The red berries all tattered and bruised,
All the nature is starting to hibernate,
And birds starting to emigrate.

The flowers begin to die away,
Shorter become the days,
The mornings are always very bleak,
The trees look very weak.

I hear the crusty, crunchy leaves being kicked around,
Everyone says they make a horrible sound,
I hear the whispering of the cold clear stream,
I can remember the warm summer in my dreams.

Autumn time has come again,
All the leaves have fallen to the ground,
Now winter has to pass around.

Sarah Dixon (12)
Carmel RC School

AUTUMN BREEZE

A merry little autumn breeze,
Whistling, rustling through the trees,
Freckled with old twigs and leaves,
Dry, crisp and broken.

Comfort in the warmth so mild,
Whistling like a joyful child,
Through the leaves so highly piled,
Happy, swirling, free.

Past the hedgehog, now well fed,
Whirling round the badger's head,
Chase the fox into its bed,
Sighing, sleeping, warm.

Cross a field, so still and bleak,
Hear the rustle of the sheep,
As they settle down to sleep,
In gentle, fading light.

See the darkness closing in,
Feel the coldness on your skin,
Hear the quiet, no more din,
In the still night air.

Blowing down a lonely lane,
Turn around, come back again!
Don't leave us to winter's reign,
Crumbled, torn and coarse.

Clare Black (12)
Carmel RC School

AUTUMN

The summer is out,
In comes autumn.
Leaves are falling off,
Colours changing to brown,
Yellow, orange and golden.
Now the leaves start
To go mouldy, decay.

Now when I look out of
My bedroom window,
All I see are leaves
In the autumn
Go away autumn please.

Now the nights are getting cold,
Now the sky is getting dull.
Now it's getting darker,
Now that summer has gone.

The weather is getting colder,
Now that winter is round the corner.
No animals about, all hibernating
For the winter.

Now people are wrapping up well
Due to the chilling wind.
Well I'm staying in to keep warm.

Now there is no football to be played,
I am bored stiff.
I hope autumn will just go away.

Nicholas Woodward (12)
Carmel RC School

AUTUMN

Red, brown, yellow, golden leaves, lovely on big tall trees.
The wind blows gently and the leaves are twisting, twirling
To the dead cold ground.

The wind comes more and more as the leaves come down.
At the end, no more leaves are left on the trees,
They lie rotten, ripped, tattered and torn.

I step outside, I can feel the ice-cold weather on my breath,
The wind bites on my nose and my toes.
I smell the winter coming near,
The nights are cutting in, the darkness arrives.
On my lawn there's a white clean sheet of snow.

Hayley Kelly (12)
Carmel RC School

HELLO AUTUMN!

How are you?
Does your gentle breeze still rustle golden leaves
That lie around the flowerless trees?

Do you (will you) still crumble under my feet?
Your golden red or dead leaves,
Your calm, dry, bare branches
Are rustling in the cool gentle breeze,
And calm me

Until the wind picks itself up.
The darkness comes like a towering big trunk.
Hello winter.
How are you?

Abigail Potter (12)
Carmel RC School

WHEN THE SEASON ENDS!

The leaves are crispy and golden-brown,
Twirling, whirling, round and round,
When I think how, how, how,
How this season has gone so fast,
Spring and summer didn't last.

From spring to summer, now autumn's here,
Did you see? How did it appear?
With the leaves so crisp and dry,
Here comes autumn, I thought I'd say 'Hi!'
Round the corner it's big old winter,
When the day finally comes, we're back to school doing sums,
When the bell rings loud and clear,
Someone shouts, 'Look! Winter's here.'
With the snow so soft and white,
We climb right up . . . to a height,
We climb the trees 'til we reach the top,
Then we look down, then it's a big drop,
The season is over, now it's spring,
Now go right ahead to the seasoning.

Emma Hall (12)
Carmel RC School

AUTUMN

A is for autumn, all the leaves on the ground,
U is for the undressing of the trees,
T is for the trees which have no leaves,
U is for umbrellas that turn inside out in the wind,
M is for the mist that swirls in the air,
N is for nuts that the squirrels collect.

Amy McLachlan (11)
Carmel RC School

PROBLEMS

Annoying blazer,
Stupid tie,
I can't get dressed,
My oh my!

Where do I go?
What do I do?
How will I find out
Who is who?

Who's in my form?
Will I make a new friend?
When will this nightmare
Ever end?

We're all walking from
Place to place,
While all these sixth formers
Think it's a race.

I feel so small in
Such a big school,
And everyone else seems to
Think it's so cool.

Bring-ding-ding,
Ring-ting-ting,
'Yes!
But where's the exit?'

Laura Brennan (11)
Carmel RC School

MY FIRST DAY AT SCHOOL

My first day at Carmel
Was like a brand-new day,
It was like a big step, in a way.
I got in my seat
Of what was now my form room,
It would be time for a lesson, really soon.
I looked around
To see all these new faces,
All of them come from different places.
'Y-y-yes Sir!'
I said when my name was read out,
I said it quietly
'Cause I didn't want to shout.
When the lesson bell rang,
We started to go,
But where we were going?
I did not know.
The school was big
With loads of doors,
And I thought I'm not small anymore.
I was stood froze
In a corridor alone,
With people like giants looking down at me as they went by,
Wondering where to go,
I walked down the long corridor,
To see people dashing through a door, going outside.
Time to go already? I thought.
So I walked outside and looked back at the big school,
I thought, today's over,
But what will tomorrow bring?

Kayleigh M Elliot (11)
Carmel RC School

MY FIRST DAY AT SCHOOL
I walk in the playground
Nobody's here.
Am I early?
Am I late?

Have I remembered everything I need?
Pencils, books, rulers, rubbers or even
Money for my dinner.

Finally somebody comes into the playground
Not worried at all.

Soon nearly everybody's here
Big children, small children.
There's about one hundred people in a
Playground.

Now I'm with my friends
I can act casual even though
Deep inside I'm scared.

The teachers are nice, happy and loud
My friends look scared, just like me.
A bell goes,
What does it mean?

Three lessons are over,
I walk down a big corridor
I see people having lunch and walking around.

I have my lunch with my friends
Knowing that this new school might just be
Fun.

Nicola Kiedish (11)
Carmel RC School

MY FIRST DAY AT SCHOOL
I got up early, with my stomach whirling,
getting dressed in my uniform, I felt proud.
I set off to meet my friends.
We all walked together, with the same cold feeling in our stomachs.
We got to school, and I saw all the familiar faces.
We laughed and joked, pretending we weren't afraid,
but we were, underneath.
We were led inside by our head of year, and met our form teacher.
He's new here too, he made us laugh.
Then break came, all the big ones, pushing through the
'little first years'.
Lunch was exciting and different.
The rest of the afternoon was quick, I kept waiting for the next break,
but none came.
At the end of the day, I walked home, and my mum was waiting for me.

Mary Doherty (11)
Carmel RC School

AUTUMN
As the wind blows through the trees at night,
It blows away a curtain of leaves,
The moon breaks suddenly from behind the clouds,
Shining down like a bright face.

When morning comes, a fog sits upon us,
As if it's waiting for something,
When it goes, it crawls slowly backwards,
Leaving behind a layer of sparkling white,
Amongst the frostbitten gardens.

Squirrels run around like leaves before a gust of wind,
The crispy gold and brown leaves crunch underfoot,
And rustle overhead, while the wind blows through
The slowly balding trees.

The birds are leaving, they're headed for the sun,
The hedgehogs make a home and hibernate away,
Autumn is here, it's nearly winter,
It's time to say goodbye to the summer sun.

Kayleigh Brown (13)
Carmel RC School

MY FIRST DAY AT SCHOOL

It felt different not being the biggest,
not knowing where to go, or who anyone is.
Learning new faces, new teachers and other children of my age,
who feel just the same as me.
Moving from class to class not knowing where to go,
or who anyone is.
Wearing a different uniform,
and checking everything is right.
Looking where to go at break,
and not knowing who anyone is.
Writing your first words on your
first book in your brand-new school.
Lining up in the dinner hall,
not knowing where to sit and then finally looking around,
at all the massive people around you.
Then finally when the last lesson has finished,
and you feel like the day's flown through,
you finally get on the bus to make that first journey home.

Thomas Craddock (11)
Carmel RC School

MY FIRST DAY AT SCHOOL

My bag was killing my shoulder,
Echoes in the hall,
Most kids big, some small,
Laughing and joking,
Shoving and pushing,
Kids get lost and then start blushing.
Got lots of homework, they say it's the law,
But I've never heard about that before.
Up the stairs for English,
My bag's breaking my back,
Eighty spellings, I nearly had a heart attack!
Almost home time, where's third break?
My head's spinning, my back aches.
Walking home with my new friends.
I have homework, like school never ends.

Francesca Appleton (12)
Carmel RC School

AUTUMN

Leaves, leaves, everywhere,
Dancing round and round,
Leaves flying high up there,
And landing on the ground.

The trees go bare with the blustery wind
And autumn is everywhere.
You always know when it's autumn
When the gold leaves drop,
And others turn yellow and brown.
The wind gets cold and very strong
And then autumn is almost gone.

Kelly Clegg (11)
Carmel RC School

MY FIRST DAY AT SCHOOL

From small to big,
How will I cope?
Teachers and children
I have a bit of hope.
Getting ready in the morning,
With my blazer and tie,
What if I get lost?
Will I start to cry?
Will the teachers be nice
At Carmel School?
Will they like me
Or think me a fool?
What if I'm late?
What will they do?
Will I get detention?
What will I do?
I'm walking to school
And everyone stares,
My mum waves goodbye
I know she cares.
The lessons were fun
And interesting for me,
I had more lessons
And then I went home for my tea.

Helen Maddison (11)
Carmel RC School

AUTUMN POEM

A utumn is a time of change, of misty mornings,
sunny afternoons, and foggy cold nights and from
the ever-changing scenery out pops robin redbreast.

U nique different colours - gold and bronze, red, orange and
russet brown, all the colours of the rustling leaves
covering the ground like a carpet from nature.

T he time for autumn has come, it's time for all the trees
to lose their leaves and as they do, all the animals
are going to sleep as winter draws ever near.

U nchanging and ever constant she visits us every year
transforming the countryside in the glorious shades of colour.
M agical, mysterious night when witches and spirits are about
and people partying at home in celebration of All Hallows Eve.
N ow autumn is nearly ending, she makes her last farewell,
trailing a few ragged leaves behind her and leaving a lonely bird
quivering as the chill of winter nears.

David Suleiman (11)
Carmel RC School

CEMETERY

Trees, twisted and bare,
Reaching for the sky.
Tearing through the darkness,
Decaying bodies, twisted within,
Rotting away.
It's so dark out there.
Run and hide,
Before we all go under.

James Doran (13)
Carmel RC School

MY FIRST DAY AT SCHOOL

I walked up the road
feeling very nervous and scared.
Trying to think about other things
- but I didn't care.
What if I fall down the stairs,
and everyone stops and stares?
What if I slip on a leaf,
and break all of my teeth?
What if I say something daft
and everyone starts to laugh?
What if I fall off my chair
and wave my legs in the air?
What if I make a mistake
and in cookery - burn my cake?
What if I have no friends,
and the day never ends?
What if I . . .

Elinor Campbell (12)
Carmel RC School

THE MOON

The moon is a big cream cracker in the sky.
Floating like a boat on a river.
He smiles down on the earth like a mother smiling at her children.
He is as peaceful as a dove and as sleepy as a lion.
He is a light bulb lighting up the sky for the stars.
He is as quiet as a mouse and as big as an elephant.
He hums to himself, all day long
Just happy to be who he is
A cream cracker - a light bulb . . .

Anna McLean (13)
Carmel RC School

MY FIRST DAY AT SCHOOL

It was my first day at school,
there I was awake at 6.30 am,
thinking about my first day.
Was it going to be a disaster,
or was it going to be great?
There I was, small little girl looking around.
Bigger people stood in crowds.
There I was wondering what to do, where to go?
We lined up ready to meet our form teacher.
First lesson I was asked 'Do you know this answer or not?'
From then on I had my ears open.
We got lost, our form teacher had to show us the way,
but he was new as well.
It was nearly home time, I was just waiting for that
clock to tick once more.
As soon as I got home and put one foot through the door
'How was your day?'
After I had told my parents, I went to my room,
I was thinking about the day, it was not that bad.
All that worry for nothing at all.

Gabrielle Browne (12)
Carmel RC School

AUTUMN IS . . .

Autumn is the swirls of icy wind
that wrap themselves around the bare branches.

Autumn is the blossom that is no longer there.
Autumn is the windy sparkles,
that lift the russet leaves,
which fade away into the distant fog.

Autumn is the squirrels,
that collect up the acorns and conkers,
for when they lay down their heads,
and drift away into the land of nowhere.

Bonfires everywhere,
red, yellow, green, blue fireworks,
shooting over the shimmering white moon.

Kate Donald (11)
Carmel RC School

MY FIRST DAY AT SCHOOL

On my first day at school, I felt like a bag of nerves,
Everyone knew what to do, where to go,
But I felt scared and alone.
Our form tutor seemed nice with a big jolly smile
and a nice smart suit,
I felt more reassured by then.
First lesson went fine,
I thought the work would be really hard,
Like everyone said,
But it was quite easy for the first day.
People told me of clubs you could go to,
They sounded great, we didn't have that at our old school.
When the end of school bell rang,
I felt happy and cheerful,
Like a heavy weight had been lifted off my shoulders,
I like high school.

Emma Parkes (11)
Carmel RC School

MY FIRST DAY AT SCHOOL

My first day at school
I tried to feel cool
As I lined up we were told to shut up!
7C walked in
And we were told to go
Into a massive assembly hall
And it wasn't small
Mr Madeley sat down
Without a frown
We walked to our room
I had nerves in my tum
We all got a seat
And sat down from our feet.

Break time came
It wasn't the same
Along came my sister
I had not missed her
10:50 came
No time for a game
We all went in
It was the middle of the day
I'm afraid to say
Soon it was lunch
Had a munch
RE after that
I think I liked that
Soon I went home
Home sweet home.

Paul Robinson (11)
Carmel RC School

AUTUMN

Autumn is coming,
Leaves swirl around in the wind in magnificent colours of
Browns, yellows, oranges and reds.
Leaves cover the bare ground,
As animals hibernate and plants die.

Trees lose their leaves and heavy showers come,
Days get shorter,
And the wind howls endlessly in the night,
The skies get dull and,
It gets colder by the day,
Berries and conkers turn ripe and fall to the ground.

But as the weeks and days go by,
Autumn is starting to come to an
End.

Michelle Tsang (12)
Carmel RC School

A HERD OF ELEPHANTS

The pupils ran along the corridor
Like a herd of elephants
Until the teacher stormed out of the classroom
And started shouting at everyone.
Then everything slowed down to a standstill
Then she started shouting
'There's a test in there!'
Then she singled out some *first year*
Out of the crowd and said
'Five past twelve - that will teach you
to run in the corridor again!'
Stephen Barningham (13)
Carmel RC School

AUTUMN

As I wake up on a morning,
I see the mist as I'm yawning.
When I open my curtains, the sparkles make me squint,
I wonder what they are,
Or maybe it's just my imagination,
Now I've realised it is autumn!

I pull on my woolly jumper,
The colours of autumn hit me,
Brown, orange, yellow, red, purple, white and blue,
All the colours I've said to you are
All the colours of autumn.

As I remember it's the 5th of November,
A loud bang snaps me out of my daydream,
I run out of the house to see the fireworks roaring,
As I realise it really is autumn!

Nadia-Ecaterina Piper (12)
Carmel RC School

AUTUMN

As I walk down the street
It's getting darker every minute
The sun is fading and the moon is rising
Leaves are falling, the wind is blowing
Them against my legs
All of a sudden I get a tingle down my spine
Just as the wind blows all over my body
And I say to myself, summer is gone, autumn is here.

Kirsty Blenkinsop (14)
Carmel RC School

MY FIRST DAY AT SCHOOL

We were all lined up
Waiting to go in
Everybody talking
Everybody nervous
Everybody excited.
You could hear the *groan* in my stomach.
I was so nervous - I didn't have any breakfast.
We finally went in for assembly.
After assembly, we went to our form rooms.
Break came . . .
I couldn't wait to have a breath of fresh air.
Break went by . . .
We went back to our form rooms
Lunch came . . .
I couldn't wait to fill up my empty stomach.
Lunch went by . . .
Music next!
Then RE
Then Geography
Geography went by . . .
Home time . . . 15.35 pm
I couldn't wait to go home and tell my mum
About the day I'd had . . .
Rachel Cassidy (11)
Carmel RC School

AUTUMN

Frost nipping at my toes,
No animals in sight,
Sharp gust of the wind gives me a little fright,
Autumn is here,
Autumn is here.

The dark comes quicker,
The rain hits harder,
Leaves fall, everything is changing quickly,
Autumn is here,
Autumn is here.

The trees are bare,
The sky turns black,
Nobody's out in the street,
Autumn is here,
Autumn is here.

Snow is now here,
The trees stay bare,
White is the colour all around us,
Autumn is over,
Autumn is over.

Gavin Swankie (13)
Carmel RC School

MY FIRST DAY AT CARMEL SCHOOL

As I stumbled onto the school bus - my stomach doing flips,
This was going to be one of my worst bus trips.
When we wandered into school we met our form tutor
and when we heard all the rules
this is a scary school!

We walked into the hall feeling very small
with teachers watching us all.
As we walked into lessons my hands were shaking
and my voice really quaking.
As I thought all the teachers had gone
a booming voice behind me said . . .
'Blazers on!'

Emma Jenkins (11)
Carmel RC School

DEVASTATION

The chugging of the engines came,
flares were parachuted down,
the siren went . . .

Everyone made a rush for the shelter,
we made it just in time.
The bombs began to stream down,
whining and screeching,
my heart was in my mouth . . .

The bombs stopped
but they didn't give up!
They came back twice as strong.
The screeching and whining louder than before.
Bricks tumbled, glass smashed,
a body thudded as it hit the ground . . .

Then silence - nothing . . .
The all-clear sounded
people streamed out.
They sobbed and wept, but I heard nothing.
I stood and stared at the sight that met my eyes.
The sight of devastation . . . !

Laura Fawcett (14)
Carmel RC School

AUTUMN

The colours of Fall.
The cracks and patterns on the frost.
The grey and cloudy thickness of the fog.
It is autumn.

The quietness of nature.
The visible breath as you breathe in the cold air.
The spiky green conkers turning brown and rotten.
It's autumn.

The crunching of the leaves walking through
the park, seeing red, brown and golden yellow.
It's definitely autumn.

Helen Richardson (13)
Carmel RC School

PRIVATE FEAR WAR ZONE

Darkness all around me
No one to be seen.
The bangs and flashes
Are getting closer.
As I run for cover
From the war zone.
The smells, the noises
Are all around me.
I'm very frightened
But try to be brave.
I feel as though
I'm all alone
Trapped inside my own war zone . . .
Luke Stott (13)
Carmel RC School

AUTUMN
The wind starting to pick up,
It's beginning to get dark,
As the cold sends goosebumps up my leg,
And the leaves fall from the trees.
It's the beginning of autumn.

The wind grows stronger,
As the sun sets in the west.
The frost gets me right on my face.
Leaves starting to hit the floor now.
It's the middle of autumn.

As the wind begins to holler,
The night is dark and silent,
As the road is like a river of ice,
But the worst is still to come in the bitter winter.
It's the end of autumn.

Robert Lambert (13)
Carmel RC School

MY FIRST DAY AT SCHOOL POEM
As I was walking to school
My heart was pounding so quick.
Everyone was so big, I felt like a fool
Everyone was taking the *mick!*
I felt like an individual walking along
To see all the children having so much fun
And then when the clock strikes half-past three
I am also very happy
And I jump around with glee . . . !
Jenna Grant (12)
Carmel RC School

AUTUMN

Autumn comes - summer goes!
The leaves change to a warm hot colour
The green leaves go.
Prickly conkers fall off the trees
They snap off with the breeze.
The mist comes with the early morning dew.
It's wet and cold.
I don't want to get out of my soft warm bed.
I let my cat out - I see smoke coming out of my mouth.
The dry crisp leaves are sleeping on the moist floor
All floppy and wet.
People stamp on them, they're sticking to their feet.
Finally the animals are starting to hibernate.
They fall fast asleep - never to wake,
But also the birds start to emigrate.
They fly away to another place.
Laura Hillyard (12)
Carmel RC School

AUTUMN

The leaves on the floor make me feel like death
They're like soldiers falling to the floor
The rain feels like bullets and the cold hits you
like a nuclear bomb

The wind is like a wall blocking your path
The snow is like a dictator making you feel in wrath
and as it sets, it sets like concrete.

The tree is now looking drastically bare
It's like an army without any men
It's fighting a war with nothing to spare
as it fights a war against autumn.

The tree is now dead having lost the war
and the leaves lie on the floor
They're like soldiers in the aftermath of a great war
Autumn is almost gone but beware
winter is still to come.

Carlo Obinu (13)
Carmel RC School

MY FIRST DAY AT SCHOOL
When I got up
I was shaking
I was quaking
'Cos it's the first day of school!
On my way to the bus stop
I was shaking
I was quaking
'Cos it's the first day of school!
I was going into lessons and
I was shaking
I was quaking
'Cos it's the first day of school!
It was time to go home
That wasn't so bad . . .
I wasn't shaking
I wasn't quaking
That's my first day . . . at school!
Rebecca Gohr (12)
Carmel RC School

AUTUMN

The golden crisp leaves that were once fresh green
are beginning to fall.
The weather which was warm and light
is becoming cold and bitter.
The ground which was full of fresh green grass
is starting to harden with the frost.
People are slowing down as the morning frosts
start to appear.
The wind is starting to whistle
around the houses.
The smoke from the coal fires
drifts down the streets.
It's getting colder every day.
Winter is soon to come . . .

Sarah Brannan (13)
Carmel RC School

THE AIR RAID

The sirens whirling
the bombs screaming down.
We ran to the shelter
and crashed through the door.
The shelter - rattling and shaking.
The bomb was close!
The guns pounding,
The planes chugging.
I knew I was safe . . .
I knew I was safe -
There was another big crash!
That's my house gone . . . !

Claire Lavender (13)
Carmel RC School

AUTUMN

The sleeping bears hide away in their caves as a refuge
from the disease of a season,
Which is slowly killing the trees.
Leaves falling all around
Changing colour then slowly falling to the ground
But nothing can stop the hibernating bear deep inside the dying earth.

As they run and rush around
Taking no time to look and find
Somewhere to sit and wait,
As this killer of a season
Flies over the earth
And the brown plague kills the very soul of our world,
The trees!

People and their modern ways,
Rushing around, not taking notice
As the world changes.
It's even happening in their homes and gardens
As the trees degrade
Turning into the brown and oranges, that autumn brings.

But don't get me wrong if I was one of you I wouldn't care too
Because I would have my warm house
But I am the squirrel
That hunts for food,
Fights for food,
Which of course,
Along with warmth,
Is only cure for the brown plague.

Daniel Stansfield (13)
Carmel RC School

THE BUBBLING STREAM

The streams were excited as they popped
out of the hole in the mountainside.
They chattered and skipped over stones in the pathway.
The stream was as clear as crystal as it slipped down with the flow.
Getting near - they started gliding over the bumps in the path.
Other streams pushed down behind them and made them trip
down the small waterfalls.
More and more streams pushed down the tiny pathway.
The stream was getting faster and bigger now.
'Faster, faster!' yelled the streams.
They were going fast now . . .
As quickly as possible down to the river.
Swishing, jolting, dodging and diving . . .
Things seemed to slow down as they approached a huge waterfall.
Whispering nervously, teeth chattering, they looked over the side!
Then an almighty push, sent them crashing down like avalanches
and into the river below!

Emma Hall (13)
Carmel RC School

AUTUMN

I wake up one morning
and look out of my bedroom window.
All I can see is rain
splashing on to the pavement.
My windows are open
and I can feel the cold air.
All I want to do is to get
a hot cuppa and a book
and snuggle down in my bed.

I sit reading my book.
I hear a knock on the door.
It's Sarah and she wants to know
if I am going out!
I say no!
Because it is really cold and damp
and then I get back into my bed
snuggle deeper down
and fall asleep . . .

Victoria Hadman (13)
Carmel RC School

WHEN WILL IT BE OVER . . . ?

The bomb makes the almighty blast they'd all been waiting for
Silence falls
Then there's angry shouts
Screaming
You can even smell the fear.
The little flowers hide away under the hedge.
Then suddenly *bang . . . thud, thud, thud . . .*
The other side are attacking back
The trees moan and the plants sigh
When will it be over?

The sun rises
Silence fills the air.
The flowers and trees pop their heads back round to
see the damage that's been done.
The wind whistles through the trees
and the birds chatter to themselves . . .

Katy Clamp (13)
Carmel RC School

AUTUMN

Crunching leaves and freezing nights
sleeping bears are sleeping tight.
Swaying leaves and colours blow
into the night - off they go!

Angry winds at soaring heights
more cold coming with every night.
Sleeping squirrels are curled up tight
summer's surrendered at autumn's fright.
ﺍ
The full moon is shining
wind below is howling and whining.
The cold is biting, it's very clear
autumn is here but we don't cheer . . .

Rebecca Eckley (13)
Carmel RC School

AUTUMN

Fall is here -
There is not a patch of green.
The sparkling frost is dripping off the trees.
There is no sign of life.
Leaves are falling like dead soldiers.
There is a creamy blanket of fog floating above the ground.
It floats around you as if it's waiting for an answer.
The hollow sound of conkers.
Dropping to the ground - it's too late
The dull death is here . . .

Craig Pickavance (13)
Carmel RC School

THE FIELD OF VIEW

Men running
'Retreat!'
Bullets whizzing past their ears.
Moans and groans
Thud!
Someone hits the ground
Bang!
A mortar being fired
'Come On!'
The Sergeant bawls
They climb back over enemy lines
Thud!
Another one falls
Bang!
This time a tank . . .
It crushes men - moaning and groaning.
Injured bodies squirm
Crash!
Bang!
Two tanks collide
Zoom!
A rocket launcher being fired
Boom!
The two tanks illuminate the sky.
Grey shadows try to flee
They are as quick as they can be
but death chases them . . . endlessly!

Carl Harpin (13)
Carmel RC School

MY FIRST THREE DAYS AT CARMEL . . .

The journey to school was long,
I felt I was going to be late.
But it passed by very quickly,
And I arrived on time with my mate!
The day went slow, but eventually,
It got to half-past three.
The bell rang, we all ran out,
Shouting 'I'm free! I'm free! I'm free!'
My second day there,
My first detention came.
I wasn't even at school,
When I got the blame!
I might have been in the wrong,
I don't even know.
But I'll not do it again,
It frightened me so!
The third day came,
My worst day of the lot.
The subjects were hard,
'Difficult or what?'
The weekend eventually came,
I felt like I was free.
I took my uniform off,
And jumped about with 'glee'!

Catherine McKeown (11)
Carmel RC School

My First Day At School

I went through the gate.
Huge and great *it* sat looming straight ahead.
It - the school!
Gloomy and half asleep in the frosty morning air.
Sitting there on the concrete
Ready to swallow you up when you walked in through the door.
And the people that filled the yard
They looked so big I felt I might be squashed by them.
Were they going to this place called *school!*
Suddenly a loud bell clanged
Like a foghorn on a ship - lost at sea.
Children began to disappear through doors into school.
Feeling a grip on my hand, I turned to see my mum
Who led me by the hand into the classroom
Into the *school*
And *into a new world . . .*

Anne Currier (12)
Carmel RC School

Autumn

Autumn is colourful with leaves and twigs on the ground
Trees are naked like soldiers dropping from a plane.
People are staying inside because of the dark, cold and windy night.
And nature is also staying inside - like a soldier retreating.

Nicholas Brydon (13)
Carmel RC School

MY FIRST DAY AT SCHOOL

Last year in *year six*
I was the biggest in my school.
But now I'm in the secondary
Standing like a fool.
I don't know where to go
I don't know who to meet.
All these things go through my head
Last night I couldn't sleep.
Finally I find a friend
But he is lost as well.
I told him I was scared
He swore he wouldn't tell.
Hundreds and hundreds of people
All know where to go.
We can't be the only ones
Who simply do not know!
We walked and walked forever
And waited by the gates.
Our eyes lit up and there we stood
Pointing at our mates.
We walked into a classroom
Then walked in a teacher.
We didn't move a muscle
Like watching a scary feature.
He called out my name
I sat there - really still.
I wanted to pass out and die
Even though I hadn't wrote a Will!
The day went quickly - the bell has gone
And all *year seven* - mark off day one!

Daniel Condren (11()
Carmel RC School

EQUALITY

Colour doesn't matter to me
I wish the world would agree
to stop all these stupid fights
that go on through days and nights.
Racism is very mean
it doesn't matter if you are blue or green.
Everyone's the same inside
so don't be shy, you have nothing to hide.
Stephen Lawrence was a kind boy
people destroyed him like a toy.
Some ghastly people took his life
with one sad blow from a knife.
Please Lord help us live together
it doesn't really matter whether
you're black or white, green or grey
we can make a difference . . . today!

Laura Sutton (11)
Fyndoune Community College

THE WHITE HORSE

I see a horse in a field, white fur like a satin sheet.
What great speed could you go
Faster and faster along the field.
The way you go on no one will know.
To the moon on this horse
Faraway planets touch the stars.
I see a horse in a field with fur like a satin sheet.
Disappears and floats away
I wish this horse was mine . . .

Diane Boyd (12)
Fyndoune Community College

MY FRIEND THE SNOWMAN

My friend the snowman
only here in snow.
Laughter, singing, coming from us
feeling merry and having fun.
But it soon ends
The sun appears
Melting my friend - every year.
Why? I ask
Does he melt
I guess I'll never know
But I know he'll be back next year
and then the fun begins again.
After that! . . . Who knows!

Helen Pinkney (11)
Fyndoune Community College

THE STONE

I come from the borders of Australia
No one lives there apart from me.
I am here to explore humans - and nothing else.
I eat something which you won't have heard of
It's delicious!
I would say I am quite intelligent
but not as intelligent as you.
You go to school - I don't!
I am as old as my tongue
and a littler older than my teeth . . .
I am so happy being around such wonderful creatures.
Leanne Bromley (11)
Fyndoune Community College

I SEARCH FOR LAND

I'm sitting in an old flimsy rotting fishing boat.
My family and lots of other people
are cramped and squashed together.
We pray for land - we pray for safety.
As I now speak, we are starving for food and drink.
We will give anything to see land again.
The people on the boat are seasick.
They are sitting by the gunwale - waiting.
We desperately search for land . . .

Melissa Sweeney (11)
Fyndoune Community College

MILLENNIUM POEM

What will the millennium be like!
Will the people still ride a bike?
Will we see aliens and robots everywhere?
If we do - would we care!
How would we dress?
What would we eat?
Strange things, I don't know.
Would we still have Zimmer frames?
Most likely . . . it will be the same!

Vicky McLaughlin (13)
Fyndoune Community College

MY SISTER ABIGAIL

My sister Abigail has blue eyes.
She likes the Teletubbies.
She's only one and likes to dance.
The words she says are *Ma* and *Da*
She has fair hair and rosy cheeks.
Very slim and loves to eat
Her favourite food is milk
You think she's cute but really she's not
Her favourite hobby is destroying things.
Abigail loves bath time
She likes to splish and splash.
It's off to bed for her,
Goodnight! Shhhhh .... she's asleep!
I don't want a peep out of her
For now!

Aimee Wilson (11)
Fyndoune Community College

OPPOSITES OF THE SHELL

I have a brain as big as the sun
Yet as small as a pin.
I am older than the sky above
Yet as young as a newborn baby.
I eat all day but am never full!
I am born a thousand times
I am everything . . . and nothing!
Victoria Bramble (11)
Fyndoune Community College

MONSTERS

Monsters creeping - silently and slow
Big teeth - big jaws - terrifying claws!
Big ones - small ones - fast and slow
They eat you for lunch - in one big munch . . .

Mark Nelles (13)
Fyndoune Community College

THE DOOMED SHIP

On its maiden voyage from Liverpool to New York,
the greatest ship in the world struck an iceberg in its path.
The proclaimed unsinkable White Star Line ship
filled with gallons upon gallons of salt water.
At a time of eleven forty five, the passengers were told
of the ship's destiny.
As desperate souls scrambled for life-boats.
One of the souls knew that there were not nearly
as many life-boats as souls - the ship's designer!
At three o'clock the following morning,
with a flash of light as the ship's engines were flooded
the lights went out and with the music of the ship's band
in the background, the once great and powerful ship was gone!
And as the few souls that watched the ship go down and break
into two, they knew there were still 1500 people on the ship
going on their voyage

To the bottom of the sea . . .
David Ellis (15)
Hurworth Comprehensive School

WIND

Wind!
Blowing through the trees
Wind!
On winter mornings making me freeze
Wind!
Howling and screeching through the night
Wind!
Whistling like a ghost, giving a fright
Wind!
Damaging buildings on a stormy evening
Wind!
Making people say *phew* when it's leaving
Wind!
Bending trees abound
Wind!
One of the worst types of weather around . . .

Peter Hedley (12)
Hurworth Comprehensive School

THE SCRAPYARD

Foul smells and oily puddles
rusty metal, rotting wood.
Old springs, empty cans,
bits of rope and pieces of string.
Patchy sofa, broken chairs,
bags of rubbish and abandoned cars.
This scrapyard is scattered with
discarded pieces of people's lives . . .
Amy Sedgwick (12)
Hurworth Comprehensive School

THE DALES

The dales in winter are covered in snow,
not even on nice days, people dare go!
You cannot tell what the weather will bring,
often the wind gets up - howls and sings.
The sheep all cosy in their woolly coats
huddle in their drystone forts.
The cosy little teashop provides shelter for the few
who have braved the elements to appreciate the view.
In the spring the hills come alive,
when the buttercups open and the ruddy ducks arrive.
The first hum of bees and the tinkling of water
spells the start of a bright new summer.
Now the moors are purple with heather,
the swallows signal a change in the weather.
The tourists come bustling through
awakening villages - small towns too.
They come to browse, paint, plod or climb
others climb aboard the Grosmont Line.
In the autumn the bracken dies
in its den the adder lies.
The red and orange crunchy leaves
flutter from moorland windswept trees.
Up on the moor, on the Pennine Way
people still trek - dusk and day.
Then as the gales and snow take hold
the sheep are gathered to their fold.
And all about the birds and animals
near to home - remain
Asleep to pass the cold dark nights away . . .

Heather Minto (12)
Hurworth Comprehensive School

THE DARKNESS OF THE NIGHT
It was the darkness of the night
everything was still.
I was shivering in my bed
as the wind was blowing through the trees,
rustling all the leaves
in the darkness of the night!

It was the darkness of the night
everything was still.
The moonlight was shining
along with the stars
through my bedroom window,
in the darkness of the night!

It was the darkness of the night
everything was still.
Just the sound of a hedgehog
walking down the street,
in all the shadows
in the darkness of the night . . .

Andrew Birkbeck (12)
Hurworth Comprehensive School

BY THE SEA
Deckchairs piled in the sand
A pier reaches from sea to land.
Castles built with a bucket and spade
Show where once the children played.

Crashing waves roll and roar
Tossing shells and pebbles towards the shore.
Beaches changing with the tide
Creating waves for the surfers to ride.

Seaweed floats amongst the rocks
And down where all the boats are docked.
Hiding there a fishy tail
Waiting for the boats to sail.

Seagulls soar towards the clouds
Then dive and cry with voices loud.
A fish or crab their meal shall be
Provided by the never-ending sea.

Jennie Haines (12)
Hurworth Comprehensive School

REPLAY OF 1966

I wasn't around when England were the greatest,
So I'm hoping for our manager's latest,
Against the Germans we've been cursed,
That's why we need a new Geoff Hurst,
With Michael Owen as England's latest.
Well there's been so many stars through the years,
There's been Robson and 'Gazza' in tears.
Peter Shilton and Glenn Hoddle,
Gary Lineker and Chris Waddle.
But they couldn't stop all these so-nears.
We've been unlucky with penalties after time,
With Pearce, Southgate and Batty responsible for these crimes.
It's like we're destined not to win,
It's like the ball just won't go in.
As the keeper saves it on the line.
At the moment we have stars in our mix,
With Sol Campbell and Beckham with his tricks.
30-odd years since we last won,
So quite soon we could have some fun
With a replay of 1966.

Adam Wilkinson (14)
Hurworth Comprehensive School

DEATH IS LIKE THE LOTTERY

Death is like the Lottery.
It always picks on those
Who least deserve it most.
The same question is always asked
Why does it have to be them?

Innocent children with sugar-coated hearts,
Beautiful people who always play their part
In helping others - whenever they can.

There is no explanation,
If there is a God
Why can't he pick on those
With hearts of stone . . . ?

There is one thought
That is nice.
God didn't have to think twice
When he picked them, one by one
He was assured perfect angels
All of them . . .

With smiles that beam across their face,
No matter how good-looking they are.
Their prettiness shows inside their hearts . . .

Kayleigh Evans (12)
Hurworth Comprehensive School

THE EVERGLADES

The Everglades is a lonely place,
With trees like crooked fingers clenched,
Casting shadows upon the murky, deep water.
The swamp gas stench bubbling up,
From the depths of the earth.
The airboats bouncing across, into the unknown,
Entering the dark and murky swamp.

Seeing only the snout of the alligator above the water,
The blurred shadow of turtles swimming beneath the surface,
The mysterious manatee lurking, looking for food,
The splashes of the little fishes emerging from the depths,
Of the spooky Everglade swamp.

Steven Wilson (13)
Hurworth Comprehensive School

THE HAUNTING OF MY GARDEN

In among the garden mist,
A hovering figure looms,
With a look of fear
She whispers words.
Then her face turns into a smile,
Then waving her hand to say goodbye
She walks away
But her gentle eyes
They will stay
In our garden
To see another day . . .

Sarah McNulty (12)
Hurworth Comprehensive School

FEELINGS

I sit here cold and alone,
No one hears my sorrow, no one hears me groan.
The day you walked out of those doors, out of my life,
it felt like the earth had tumbled down over me.
Your smile will always be with me, as well as the
memories that are engraved into my heart, of you.
You are someone special, I know I'll never find another you.
To hold you,
To feel you,
To keep us together,
To kiss you,
To need you,
Is what I'd wish forever,
To hold you, is to need you,
To feel you, is to love you,
For us to stay together is
just so impossible.
All those things above
are what we need for this crazy
love affair to ever continue.

Sarah-Jane Brown (14)
Hurworth Comprehensive School

SUMMERTIME

The sun is scorching in the sky,
I jump and laugh,
It's summertime

Beaches, playgrounds,
Here we come,
Summertime, is such fun.

T-shirts, shorts,
Are all we see,
Children laughing joyfully.

Animals are born,
Plants come out,
It's summertime without a doubt!

Emma Graham (12)
Hurworth Comprehensive School

WHISPERED STORIES TOLD ME ABOUT THE SEA
Whispered stories told me,
of mermaids and mermen,
flowing seaweed hair.
Of undersea laughter with dolphins playing,
peaceful seabeds and vibrant coral reefs.
Of the whales awaking,
having a treat on small tiny fish.
Of stingrays and jelly-like-fish,
with shimmerful colours.
Of fish and vibrant sea colours,
dancing around rocks.
Of peaceful seashores on a deserted island,
all the peace of this land.
Of the interruption of the sea,
as an octopus appears.
Of the kill of the fish,
blood is shed.
Of the silence of this land,
as the sand slowly settles.
Of the sharks clearing this mess,
all the blood and the rest.

Laura Louise Foers (13)
Hurworth Comprehensive School

WILL THE WORLD . . . ?

A few things I want to know.
Will the earth blow up and go?
Will the world be computerised?
And will we all get miniaturised?

Did God know what he was making
For the seven days he was creating?
Will Jesus come back alive?
If he does, will he survive?

Will people whiz around in electrocars?
And will there be holidays on Pluto and Mars?
What will it be like in the year 2001?
Will we be here or will we be gone?

Holly Avery (12)
Hurworth Comprehensive School

STOP!

Stop it now, before it's too late,
Before they disappear off the face of the earth.
Another creature gone?
We can't let it happen.
So *stop,*
Before the tiger is just another animal
Extinct forever.

Stop killing the tiger,
Just let it be,
For future generations,
So they can see.

Laura Bernstone (14)
Hurworth Comprehensive School

THE BEACH

As I walked onto the beach
my feet were tickled by the heat.
Surfer being carried by the waves.
Little children laughing and playing.

The rocks so ugly yet beautifully shaped,
by the crash of the waves.

Sandcastles standing perfectly,
after being so carefully built.
The sea creeping upon every wave,
bringing the sandcastle down.
As the sun starts to set,
people begin to leave.
Like their shadows on the sand.

Now the sand is cold as the night falls,
leaving the beach alone again.

Chris Harrison (12)
Hurworth Comprehensive School

THE SETTING OF THE SUN

The sun setting with golden colours,
Brightening the dark blue sky.
The sea slowly swallowing the fiery ball,
Into its murky depths.

The sea crashing on the rocks,
Then slowly moving back to where it belongs.
The gulls swooping over the sea,
Before flying to the cliffs for the night.

Nichola Ingledew (12)
Hurworth Comprehensive School

A Poem About An Old Lady Named Lorna

There is an old lady,
who lives round the corner,
she is so friendly,
and her name is Lorna.
She walks down the street,
with a bag on her arm,
cheerfully smiling and keeping people calm.
She shouts 'Hello' and 'How are you?'
giving out sweets to the children too.
Every Wednesday at half-past ten,
she fills in her lotto ticket with a silver pen.
When she gets home,
she's all alone.
She's the nicest old lady I've ever known.

Clare Blacklee (13)
Hurworth Comprehensive School

Sun

A great burning ball
dazzling you with light.
A fire of lava
red, orange and yellow.
Like a ball of golden chain
twisted and twined together.
Like the colour of autumn leaves
rustling on the ground.
Hiding behind fluffy white clouds
disguising its beauty.

Gemma Harris (12)
Hurworth Comprehensive School

THIS IS LOVE

Through the wind,
Sun and rain,
Through the heartbreak and pain,
You are with me,
This is love.
Through the good times,
And the bad,
Through the hard and the sad,
You are with me,
This is love.
Through the torment and tragic,
Through the danger and magic,
You are with me,
This is love.
Through the good and bad weather,
We will always be together,
You are with me,
This is love.
We're together,
Forever,
Until death do us part,
I will carry you forever,
You will live in my heart.

Laura Todd (12)
Hurworth Comprehensive School

HIROSHIMA

Hiroshima
City of peace
Home for millions
Hiroshima
The great Japanese city
A lovely place to live
Hiroshima
The scenery so alluring
The countryside picture-perfect
Hiroshima
High-rise buildings, so easily flattened
The bomb drops, complete devastation
Hiroshima
The lifeless city.

Robert Lawrence (15)
Hurworth Comprehensive School

TRUE LOVE

Crystal-clear water,
The full moon above,
The couples below,
Very much in love.

Roses and candles,
In the restaurant nearby.
The holding of hands,
And the love-bitten sighs.

Down on one knee,
A young man goes.
To a young lady,
He wants to propose.

They leave together,
Hand in hand,
They should be together forever,
With true love until the end.

Toni Leach (12)
Hurworth Comprehensive School

NO ONE CARES ABOUT THE THIRD WORLD COUNTRIES

The Third World situation's getting worse,
even as I write this verse.
People suffering, people dying,
do something about it? No one's trying.

Suffering people on the street,
pacing for hours in the sun, no shoes on their feet.
The nearest water miles away,
to get there and back takes almost a day.
By that time the only water they've got,
has been boiled in the baking sun, so hot.

Children are crying with the hunger pain,
crop farmers are sitting and praying for rain.
Families trying to get over their loss in vain,
of a diseased family member dying again.

Why does no one help them? Why does no one care?
The answer's quite simple . . . 'The Third World is quite rare . . . '
No it isn't, something needs to be done,
the crisis that's going on out there, could happen to anyone.

Nicola Foster (14)
Hurworth Comprehensive School

ARMAGEDDON

The dust settles,
Machines stand still
And the world, stays silent

The black clouds speed across the sky
And the sunlight is blocked
All life is dead
And for what?

A quest for land and power
A search for the ultimate strength
Which was found in nuclear power

It was the ultimate power,
The ultimate weapon
In the hands of the ultimate killers
Leading to ultimate destruction

In the hands of politicians,
Who would have guessed
One little skirmish,
Would grow into this?

Phillip Sievers (14)
Hurworth Comprehensive School

THE DEEP, DARK WOODS

In the deep, dark wood,
Where the trees are grey,
And the mist hangs low to the ground,
There are winds that howl,
And no light to be seen.
Out in the deep, dark woods.

In the deep, dark wood,
Where the trees are grey,
And the mist hangs low to the ground,
There are owls that hoot,
And shadows that move.
Out in the deep, dark woods.

Kati Hayllar (13)
Hurworth Comprehensive School

HAVE YOU EVER STOPPED TO THINK?

Have you ever stopped to think about others besides yourself?
Have you ever stopped to notice the Third World's cry for help?
Have you ever stopped to think about what's going on around?
Poor people starving and the dying children's screaming sounds.
Wars raging throughout our world, people just don't care,
About the human beings affected, I don't know how they dare.
What's the point in fighting?
What difference will it make?
They only think of victory,
Not the precious lives they take.
How can people actually murder,
With their sick and thoughtless minds,
Do *they* stop to think about the family left behind?

Maybe in the future, a long, long time away,
Humans may come to realise that we are here to stay.
We weren't made for fighting, murdering or polluting the earth,
Our reason was to live our life and show God what we're worth.
If we want to live in peace,
Do it . . . before it's too late.

Vickie Robinson (14)
Hurworth Comprehensive School

THE NOISE

I hear a noise,
Every day I hear the noise,
Now it's started getting louder,
I know they're getting closer.

I can't sleep,
The noise is no longer a murmur,
I hear guns firing,
And I hear people screaming.

I smell smoke,
My village is on fire,
I have to run,
I have to get to safety.

I hear footsteps,
They're coming for us,
We have to run again,
I look for somewhere to hide.

I spot a hole,
I can just fit in it,
I wait for them to go,
They pass by me.

It's dawn,
The sun's rising,
I climb out of my hole,
And walk to my village.

I see nothing but ashes,
It's all gone,
Even the people,
I sit and I cry.

Nicola Fullard (12)
Hurworth Comprehensive School

I AM ALONE

It's out there, I can feel it,
It's getting closer
Soon people will be screaming.
The ground will shake and shudder,
I can see people dying,
The ground collapsing.
No!
I must stop thinking,
I am safe
But I'm alone.
I want people around
Laughing and having fun.
But I don't,
I am alone
With no one else
In the world.

Kelly Pybus (13)
Hurworth Comprehensive School

THE BEREAVEMENT

Close your eyes and bite your tongue,
This feeling will be forever young.
A young person's life has slipped away,
Everyone says someone must pay.
Something good or maybe bad,
She was the best friend I'd ever had.

Gemma Roberts (12)
Hurworth Comprehensive School

ONE SECOND OF LIFE
From the moment I checked into a packed and sealed life,
Half-prepared on the factory line,
A mechanical mentor taught false conformist values,
Forced then into an unwilling soul.
As young I loved unquestioning
Playing in manufactured false fields
The fake plastic trees whistled round my head,
Was I feeling content?
As years went by, values went stale,
Data scrambled,
Lost identity.
Was I insane, was sanity sane?
Was I the last sanity?
Conformers passed in their scripted lives
How could they go on this way?
I tell, they don't listen,
Too busy faking emotion.
They had to go, I had to release them
From their mental shackles,
Their government-controlled lives ended
I had helped, or had I? Did I have to go?
It was wrong. I left for the bridge.
I sat high above the mannikin
On my stony perch, one fall and it was over
These years of battles with false identities
Were complete with one second of life.
A fall? A jump?
A second? A lifetime?
I know I had broken free from this non-life.
For a second, my lifetime, my second of life.

Chris Devlin (14)
Hurworth Comprehensive School

NIGHT

Night wraps herself around the earth,
Smothering us with her velvet cloak,
Shielding us from the sun's unrelenting glare.
The stars shine merrily like diamonds in the sky,
Oblivious to the people that lie sleeping below,
The moon casts her shadow across the earth,
Bathing the land in an eerie light.
Everything is still,
Watching, waiting,
Will the sun rise again?

As the sun stretches her scorching fingers,
The moon bows her head for another day,
Until the night comes again.

Sarah Welch (15)
Hurworth Comprehensive School

THE SNOW OWL

The snow owl
white as can be.
Softer than snow,
swoops down
catching defenceless prey
as fast as a human eye.
Big wings spread
like a jumbo jet.
Sharp claws grab
soft feathers.
Like a pillow on a bed.

Sean Lamb (12)
Hurworth Comprehensive School

CHRISTMAS

Christmas is a lovely time,
Trees lit up all over the place.
Children singing happy songs,
About Santa's happy smiling face.

Presents under the Christmas tree,
Next to a big glowing fire.
Wrapped up are all the games,
Of which the children never seem to tire.

Cards being passed out,
Which make the room glow.
But the one thing I look forward to,
Is the white flaky snow.

Lauren Drysdale (14)
Hurworth Comprehensive School

AUTUMN

Autumn is,
The crisp brown leaves,
That float,
Downwards onto the dew-covered hedges,
Which plays a host to the dusty ground,
That lies flat beneath the skeleton trees,
And allows the tarnished trunk a place,
To give a home to all its naked dying bones,
That lose their flesh to autumn's breeze,
Of whom gives the leaves their souls to rest,
Upon the changing season's breast.

Alex Minto (14)
Hurworth Comprehensive School

WHY?

Months of pure happiness
Where has it gone?
We used to cherish our time together
Now it's just routine.
You used to bring surprises
Every Sunday at 3pm.
You'd pick me up and waiting for me
Was he next in my collection of presents.

Meals out all over the place
Nothing was too much trouble.
So thoughtful, not like the others.
You told me I was the best thing ever
And I told you how I loved you.

But then, one night, one dance, one kiss.
That one kiss that meant nothing to anyone else
Meant everything to me.
My heart dropped and now still hasn't risen fully.

Why, oh why, did you treat me so right
Then do something so wrong.
Will it ever be the same
With my first love?

Pippa Baker (15)
Hurworth Comprehensive School

SPACE: VOLUMINOUS NOTHINGNESS
Space,
what is this place?
The never-ending nothingness
that goes on forever.
Or is there a barrier which we cannot sever.

Is space just the glistening of stars?
Or does life thrive on planets like Mars?
Does space just end?
Or is it infinity?
Thoughtful people have thought to insanity!
Are we the first life?
Or are we the last?
Is the existence of others buried in the past?
I don't know,
I don't think I ever will.
But there must be something more beyond our window sill.
Philip Masters (14)
Hurworth Comprehensive School

WHAT IS OLD?
What is old?
Old is like a book that's nearly finished,
It's like you're at the core of an apple,
Like a journey that's nearly ended,
A prisoner who's almost done their time.

What is old?
Old is like a clock that's ticked all it can,
It's like a pen that's almost run out,
Like a battery that's lost its power,
A printer that's nearly run out of ink.

Emma Samuels (14)
Hurworth Comprehensive School

WITHOUT YOU

It's lonely,
It's heartbreaking,
It's depressing,
Without you.

I'm crying,
I'm hurting,
I'm lost,
Without you.

I'm alone,
With nobody,
Only memories,
Of you.

What would it take
For you to come back,
Into my life?
I love you.

Emma Todd (14)
Hurworth Comprehensive School

STRESSED

You see parents in supermarkets,
The kids are running wild,
The adults screaming and shouting,
Trying to control the child.

Adults driving in traffic jams,
Swearing and shouting, beeping the horn,
Children in the passenger seat,
The kiddies' seat is torn.

And just when they think it's all over,
And they sit in a chair for a rest,
The babies starts screaming and bawling,
No wonder adults are stressed!

Victoria Chisholm (14)
Hurworth Comprehensive School

SHARKS IN THE SEA

In the depths of the sea,
The Great White rules like a king.
The whale shark is the biggest shark yet,
Getting as much as he can get.
He looks like a plane in flight,
But hard to see at night.
The reef is home to lots of fish and sharks,
Fish are not safe from them.
The coral reef is like an underwater paradise,
Rays are up to 20m at the most.
Skates' eggs are like burnt toast,
The ray is a cousin to the shark.

Anthony Scott (11)
Hurworth Comprehensive School

THE BATTLE

Men and soldiers off to war
Their wives are waving from the door.
Off they go with all their armour
To scare away the Spanish Armada
Here they are now in the battle
Their swords and shields making a rattle.
In the water on the land
Dying men are holding hands
Ships are sinking, men are dying
Women and children are now crying.
The ships have sunk, the men have drunk
Those who are left, go home.

Christopher Hedley (12)
Hurworth House School

THE AUTUMN WEATHER

As the wind blows against the trees,
the leaves come tumbling down.
The leaves scatter on the path,
making a path of leaves.
Brown, orange and yellow are the autumn colours.
As you or I walk across the path,
crunch and crinkle are the sounds you seem to hear.
The sky is full of delightful colours,
like greys, oranges and deep reds.
Autumn is a colourful time of year.

James Gale (12)
Hurworth House School

THE POOL

So smooth and cool,
Is the echoing pool,
I feel so excited,
When I jump in the water,
No other feeling could be so soothing
As the echoing pool.

When I dive in,
I feel like a pin,
So smooth and streamlined,
Sinking to the bottom,
When I surface I feel fine,
In the echoing pool.

Martin Nichols (12)
Hurworth House School

HORSE RIDING

Happy when you sit in the saddle
Orienteering around the forests
Racing like a steam train
Spooky when rain falls
Enjoyable when it's sunny
Really enjoyable
I would like it if we did a lot of jumping
Doing nothing is boring
Incredibly athletic
Nice to ride the pony that you want to.
Great, excellent!

Richard Phillips (11)
Hurworth House School

BIRDS
Bluebirds flying over the mountains
Ibis wanders with long legs
Red robins, sitting here and there
Ducks, ducking and diving everywhere
Swans, swimming gracefully in a pond.

Jonathan White (12)
Hurworth House School

UNDER THE SEA
Splosh, through the coral I see
shimmering fish in all shapes and sizes.
Down, down I go, now I see grey
white shark in the distance,
now riding on a giant manta ray in its
underwater world.
Down, down I go.

Miles Newton (12)
Hurworth House School

THE SCARECROW
I am a scarecrow,
I live on a hill in rain, sunshine and snow,
My clothes are all ragged,
I am not meant to be smart,
My job is to scare the birds,
They eat the seeds when they dare,
But I stand out to scare.

Matthew Gale (12)
Hurworth House School

THE FOREST

The leaves in the forest are bright
It's dark in the forest at night
The birds in the forest sing songs
The claws on the owl are long
The wonderful colours and noises all round
The crackle of leaves make a crunching sound
The slimy snake and wild boar
The tiny insects on the floor
All British animals live happily there
Apart from the Australian koala bear.

Alex Strachan (12)
Hurworth House School

FIREWORKS

A Roman candle is such a sight,
Spurting out beautiful colours into the night sky.
Red, blue, white, crimson,
Exploding with plumes of colour.
Then suddenly it stops and fades away.

The Catherine wheel starts
Spinning faster and faster.
Sparks flying everywhere,
Will it ever stop? Hopefully not.

The match hits the wick of the banger
Whoosh, it flies off with great speed.
Then *bang!* It explodes making people jump.

The squealer shoots off into the night sky,
Screaming until it explodes in a plume of colours.

Kris Suddick (12)
Moorside Comprehensive School

FIREWORKS

C atherine wheel is the first one lit.
A nd round she goes fast, and she also spits.
T he children fixed on her as she squeals.
H er voice sounds like screeching wheels.
E verlasting, she goes round and round.
R eady to explode, making a banging sound.
I n the end she flies up high.
N ow she's soaring through the sky.
E yes fixed on her all the time.

W hee, whooshing into space,
H er body's full of elegance and grace.
E veryone's still waiting for her to explode.
E ventually it happens, she's made the loudest bang.
L eaving the sky all colours, the main one green,
    She's the best firework anyone has ever seen.

R eady for take-off 5, 4, 3, 2, 1.
•   ff it takes, now it's gone.
C olours flying in the sky.
K eeping their eyes on the colours as they fly by.
E veryone's cheering now it's in the air.
T hen it bangs and everyone gets a scare.

F izzing, flashing,
O ut the sparklers come.
U nder, over, they jump about.
N o one knows when they're going to stop coming out.
T he eyes are watching it all the time.
A nd how I wish it was mine.
I n the end the sparks die off.
N one left but don't worry there'll be some more.

Abbie Whitehead (12)
Moorside Comprehensive School

A POEM FOR MY SISTER RACHEL

No matter what, you're on my mind,
Not a dearer friend could anyone find.
Your smile, your laugh, the way you talk,
How could anyone forget your own special walk?
Never once did I hear you complain,
Never angry, or cause anyone pain.
I'll always picture your sweet friendly smile,
To see it again, I'd walk a million miles.
A beautiful flower, always in bloom,
Your presence would brighten any dark room.
When I look back and see your sweet face,
Happy memories of you are all that takes place.
Never has there been a chirpier friend,
I'll carry these memories right to the end.
A beautiful place, I picture you there,
In heaven with angels and people who care.
Now and forever a place you deserve,
A friend forgotten . . . *never.*

Jessica Maughan (12)
Moorside Comprehensive School

ON BONFIRE NIGHT

On Bonfire Night I was hanging around,
waiting for light and unearthly sound.
Then out of nowhere it began to roar,
like an animal no one had seen before.

The whistlers began to howl and squeal,
and someone lit a Catherine wheel.
Round and round and round it goes,
when it stopped I wouldn't know.

The sky lit up with yellow and blue,
red and pink and orange too.
The rockets exploded with a bang
and all was quiet till the whistlers sang.

They howled and screamed, we gasped below
we looked in amazement at the spectacular show.
It shot up again just like before,
and stayed up there forever more.

Gregg Allaker (12)
Moorside Comprehensive School

FIREWORKS

The bonfire is lit as we come from home
As the grey misty smoke rises to the sky.
Old people get cold and start to moan
The feathers of ash float into everybody's eyes.
They explode with many different coloured showers
That shine upon this night.
The rocket has many powers
This firework gives us all delight.
The banger bangs in the sky
It gives us a fright.
Little kids start to cry
As the banger bangs tonight.
The Catherine wheel whizzes round
This is the best firework yet.
Colours fly off not making a sound
We see this again as it's a yearly event.
Kirsty Grant (12)
Moorside Comprehensive School

FIREWORKS

All is quiet until it glitters
It's gone, disappears at first,
Then the bang is heard
Sparks and colours glow into the night.
Twists and turns, the colours are bright
Thousands of lights fly
Up, up, up - into the night
It stopped - where did it go?
A sudden spark, a ring of colours.
Amazing twists and twirls with all its might
Flying into the darkness
Sparks detach and fall to the ground.
Millions of glittery stars appear
The crowds started shouting
Exploding stars fall and it's over
Looking forward to it - next year . . . !

Kerry Mordue (12)
Moorside Comprehensive School

FIREWORKS

Catherine wheels are so much fun.
Watching, you can see the sun.
Swirling, twirling, round they go,
Turning sounds like feet in snow.

Sparklers are crackling wands,
One for each and everyone.
Write your name in pitch-black sky,
Lots of good fun that never dies.

Racing through the night sky,
Over the hills as it cries.
Soaring up so high,
Up and up, into the sky.

Colours burning in the air,
Bang! Pop! Boom! I wonder where?
A banger is like a shooting star,
Coming to you from afar.

Leanne Elliott (12)
Moorside Comprehensive School

BONFIRE NIGHT DELIGHT

A freezing cold and windy night.
November 5th is Bonfire Night.
The fireworks are ready, ready to be lit,
You'd better watch out, stand back a bit!
The rockets up high in the sky
'Look at that!' the people cry.
Roman candles spit and spark
Sparklers light up in the dark.
The bonfire's lit, flames so bright.
Glowing warmly in the night.
We crowd around the burning flames
Come and join our fun and games.
At last it's over, the bonfire's out.
'We want more!' the children shout.
We've had our fun, there is no more
Come back next year - when the fire will roar!
Kirstin McGuigan
Moorside Comprehensive School

FIREWORKS

Stood there still upon a stand,
The Catherine wheel looked lonely, but somehow grand,
Suddenly a fantastic sight,
The Catherine wheel sparked to life,
Like a bicycle wheel going fast
It gradually slowed to breathe its last.
Whizzz . . . and up it soared
The rocket roared.
The sound died down - but what a fright!
Bang . . . and what a sight!
Thousands of sparklers filled the sky
They landed on the grass around
And gradually the glow died down.
I spun around and heard a noise,
I saw some mischievous-looking boys.
They lit a banger and up it went
I heard a gunshot - before the descent!
I looked up to the fence and gave a sigh
I saw a flame 10 feet high
Like a furnace, big and bright
The fireworks read
. . . Goodnight . . .

Stephen Westgarth (12)
Moorside Comprehensive School

FIREWORKS

There I stood on Bonfire Night, without a firework in sight,
but a cone shape upon the floor,
just sat there, then I heard the roar,
a fountain of colours burst out of the top,
yellow and blue, it had the lot.
Close behind came indigo and the glowing
patterns of the volcano.

Up it went soaring into the night,
its loud, whoosh gave a fright.
Like a glowing ball flying into space.
as if it was trying to win a race, blue, gold or maybe red,
with the stars along, the rocket sped,

Twirling colours as soon as it's lit,
it makes you dizzy just watching it.
The Catherine wheel spins round and round,
without even making a sound.
Its dazzling colours light up the night,
just seeing it is such a delight.

Shooting up to the sky, it flies so high
then I heard a sudden bang.
It was the banger, banging so loud,
banging once and banging twice and banging once again.
All the showering colours each take a different lane.
Now I must go, but don't despair for I'll be back next year.

Callie O'Brien (12)
Moorside Comprehensive School

FIREWORKS ALIGHT

When ignited, flies round and round
When burnt out - starts slowing down.
All colours shoot off its tail
The Catherine wheel will never fail.

Watch it take off up into the night,
Having burnt out, disappears from sight.
Colours start, in the sky they hang
The rocket ends in one big bang.

Watch the welding fire start
Leading up into one big spark.
I'll go out now I would reckon
Hold a sparkler - wait one more second.

Placed in a hole in an old tree stump
When ignited, takes off with a thump.
It spreads out in one big flower
The lights fall down
Cascading in a shower . . .

Kirsty Baum (12)
Moorside Comprehensive School

THE T-REX

The man eating monster from hell
Makes slightly less noise than a bell.
When he's creeping up on his prey
But his prey is running away.

The Tyrannosaurus Rex stands looming
Its teeth and hands could do with a clean.
It spends its days just hunting and scaring
The grips and claws on its feet not wearing.

Just think of all the towns and cities
Where we live, we'd be full of pity.
If he was here to spend a day
He'd rip us to bits . . . we would pay!

Jemma Green (12)
Moorside Comprehensive School

FIREWORKS

Standing near the bonfire warm and bright,
Catherine wheels swirling, twirling right.
Squealing, popping, banging like mad
Shining like a bright star had.
Rockets launching into space
Rising then popping - greens, yellows, pinks exploding.
Sounds like bombs booming
Calming as they touch the ground.
Bright colours coming out of the crater,
Volcanic eruption is awaiting.
Sparking, zooming, low on the ground
Brighter colours all around.
Star shining brightly on the ground
A Roman candle burning out loud.
Shooting high in the air
Exploding while it is there.
Fireworks over for this year
Hope you will be there next year.
Lyndsay Morecroft (12)
Moorside Comprehensive School

FIREWORKS

As the rocket firework
Shoots into the night,
The colours so blinding
What a wonderful sight.
The volcano spits
And shoots like a kite
Hissing and spitting
With all its might.
Different shades
Too hot to handle
From a Catherine wheel
To a Roman candle.
The colours so bold
The colours so bright.
Orange and red
And blue and white.
Bang it goes
Such a sound it made.
Then quickly and
Suddenly . . . *it faded away!*
Dawn Whaley (12)
Moorside Comprehensive School

NOVEMBER THE 5TH

Moon rocket
The moon rocket scans the ground.
It takes to the ground like a craze
It explodes with a weird sound
They all scream - amazed!

Rocket
The rocket shoots into the sky
Everyone stares
The colour seeps in their eyes
Everyone glares!

Blue Pearl
It shoots up in the sky
Then it dazzles
Then it hits the guy
The guy now frazzles.

Catherine wheel
The Catherine wheel spins
It lights and sparks
Then the fun begins
Amazement in the park . . . !

A Brewis (12)
Moorside Comprehensive School

A BOX OF FIREWORKS

A box of fireworks
What a sight!
Soon they'll be
Burning in the night.
The Catherine wheel
It spins round and round.
It's spitting out colour
With a cracking sound.
Light the rocket
Watch it fly.
As it shoots up loudly
Into the sky.
A big loud bang
Fills the air.
A boy with a banger
Creating a scare.
Children with sparklers
Blue, red and green.
The best fireworks
That I've ever seen . . . !

Jemma Richardson (12)
Moorside Comprehensive School

NOVEMBER THE 5TH

5, 4, 3, 2, 1 - blast-off into the sky.
Like a shooting star
A trail of stardust sparkling through the sky
Mission abandoned . . .

A shy child standing in the corner,
While everyone runs around.
A fountain of sparkles - a single flame
Only a whisper of sound . . .

An alien spacecraft round and round
It never stops - keeps firing!
Aliens here - they can't stay long
Sparks of colour and soon they're gone.

Sparklers of magic in your hand
Writing your name in the dark.
November the 5th - the night of fire
Your sparklers are lit
It's time for the fun to begin . . .

Kirsten Shipley (12)
Moorside Comprehensive School

THE FOUR SEASONS
In autumn leaves turn red and gold.
Drifting down to the floor.
Squirrels gather nutty supplies
Then hide them in a store.
Winter creeps up
With snow that's bright.
Every field is a blanket
of white . . .
Spring occurs carrying a fresh new breeze
A cargo of green leaves to fill up the trees.
Summer attacks armed
with a white hot sun.
Ice cream to share
and seaside fun . . .
Sarah McGough (12)
St John's RC Comprehensive School, Bishop Auckland

STARS
I see the stars above me
I know which one is you.
You are the brightest one
And the brightest person I knew.
I miss you day by day
The love we shared in every way.
You will always be remembered
By every person you knew.
No one could ever forget you
That would be untrue.

Hayley Jane Sullivan (12)
St John's RC Comprehensive School, Bishop Auckland

THE BONFIRE

They came from near
They travelled from far.
They rambled on foot
They journeyed by car
To see the bonfire burn . . .

Originally, just a pyramid of twigs,
It expanded and swelled and got quite big,
Until at last the time was right
The people assembled at the site
To behold the bonfire burn . . .

At first, only a tiny spark
That flickered bright into the dark.
Then whoosh - the flames climbed high
And lightened up the darkened sky
As they watched the bonfire burn . . .

The flames of orange, red, yellow and blue
Made up that wonderful spectacular hue.
The smoke swirled up into the night
To take away the stars so bright
As they observed the bonfire burn . . .

The flames diminished, the warmth now gone.
Nearly over now - it won't be long!
The Guy in fragments in the embers
The people leave but will remember
When they watched the bonfire burn . . .

Richard Simpson (12)
St John's RC Comprehensive School, Bishop Auckland

MY FAVOURITE PLACE

In our garden sits a huge tree, a place where I always long to be.
The leaves are all rusty, the ends are all crusty.
They were lovely and green but now they are brown.
During the day you can't get me down!
The branches are thick, the leaves are so fine.
At night, through my window - I see them shine.

My friends love to play up and down the tree.
I stay down while leaves fall on my knee.
Suddenly it starts to snow, all my friends are told to go.
I go inside and watch TV then the sun comes out after my tea.
The snow has melted, the grass is all dry.
So I climb to the top and pretend I can fly!

Every day I like to climb, because it's the only time
When I can relax and think things through.
This tree is the best, I think you'll agree
I'm very lucky to have this tree.
I bet you wish you were like me . . . !

Laura Gowland (12)
St John's RC Comprehensive School, Bishop Auckland

BED!

In bed at last after a long hard day.
My own private space to pass the time away.
Alone I sit to read my book
In my cosy quiet nook.

As I finish turning the pages,
I realise I've been reading for ages.
Suddenly the door opens; my mum gives me a frown
So I put the book down.

I extinguish the light, snuggle under the cover
Say good-night to my mother.
I drift off to sleep and dream
About all the things . . . I have seen!

Simon Temby (12)
St John's RC Comprehensive School, Bishop Auckland

THE GIGANTIC JUNGLE
The gigantic mighty jungle
as tropical as can be.
Not that I would want to live there
because there's not very many things to do!
The gigantic mighty jungle
danger all around.
Predators are hunting for food to survive
so don't get too close or they'll eat you!
The gigantic mighty jungle
torrential and humid in different places.
You can drive around all day in a boat
and see nature that's all around you.
The gigantic mighty jungle
as wild as can be.
Sometimes bedlam, sometimes tranquillity
so beware if you travel there!
Carl McGregor (12)
St John's RC Comprehensive School, Bishop Auckland

HOLIDAY

Holiday, holiday!
Time for fun.
We're off to the beach
to lie in the sun.

With our towel and shades
we'll have great days.
Go surfing on the waves
and swimming in the sea.
This has been the holiday for me.

Go back to the apartment
to eat great meals.
With our tongues all hot
we'll try not to shout.

When we've finished
we'll have a rest.
When we awake
we'll go and get dressed.

When we're dressed
we'll run downstairs,
to find our friends
to go and play.

When we've played
we'll go back upstairs,
to see our family and friends
and when we've said our last goodbyes
it will be time to
Fly . . . fly. . . fly!

Anthony Bowes (12)
St John's RC Comprehensive School, Bishop Auckland

THE FIRST DAY OF SPRING

I wake up to sounds of newly-born birds,
singing outside my window.
Parents out looking for worms,
hatchlings chirping for food.
When parents return, they feed their young,
but not in a normal way.
They bend over, open their mouths,
are sick down the babies' throats.
Down on the ground, lie diamonds of dew,
glistening in the sun.
Dazzling sunshine shines through the clouds
onto frosted grass.
All around the garden, in fields too
are first sprouting buds, some have blossomed.
Neighbours are happy, so am I.
My parents are smiling, I think they are ill.
Snow has now gone,
suntan's on its way.
Nights become lighter
temperatures rise.
Smiles on people's faces stretch from ear to ear.
Postmen are whistling loud as trains.
Newly-sprouted daffodils surround the house.
Shining gold centres dazzle your eyes.
Summer will soon be here,
holidays start . . .

Adam Blenkinsop (12)
St John's RC Comprehensive School, Bishop Auckland

WEATHER

Rain, rain - go away!
Don't come back
Be dry all day.
Sun, sun - burning bright
Stay right there
What a gleaming sight.
Thunder rumbles
Lightning crumbles.
Wind blows
Water flows.
Toes freeze
Shaking trees.
Weather, weather!
I don't know
Stay here
Or simply go . . .

Richard Morley (12)
St John's RC Comprehensive School, Bishop Auckland

JUNGLE ANIMALS

In the jungle we hear
noisy monkeys chattering away
While the hungry tiger hunts his prey.
The rustle of the leaves are all
that gives him away . . .

Snakes slithering in long green grass,
flickering red tongues tasting the air.
A glare in their eyes,
they hope to surprise.

Thumping sounds of the herd,
echo through the jungle.
Their long trunks,
swaying from side to side.
Young calves left way behind.

Birds hunting for insects they desire
Warm humid tropical air attracts
many creatures there.
Animals compete in this jungle fair . . .

Emma Barker (12)
St John's RC Comprehensive School, Bishop Auckland

LION

Powerful lion searches innocent, defenceless prey.
Something to fill his mate, their young.
Vulnerable young tiger cub crosses his path,
Lion waits until cub is quite a way onto his patch
then pounces . . . !

Cub puts up quite a chase at first
until they arrive at bare, dry Savannah,
Where lion gains ground on tiring cub,
it is now obvious that both runners are slowing.
However is it a clever scheme set up by lion
to fool confident cub?
As now I see him once more beginning to sprint.
He leaps onto small cub and bites huge chunks of his legs.
Poor, phenomenally deformed cub is dragged to lion's den
Where it is brutally savaged for the sake of
the lion's survival . . . !

Hannah Daltry (12)
St John's RC Comprehensive School, Bishop Auckland

IT'S A FISH'S LIFE . . .
Far down in the depths of the deep blue sea,
lives a fish as big as me!

With a feather-like tail
and a shark-like fin!
When he opens his mouth
he gives a big grin.

He's green and blue
with speckles of red.
A rock - his house,
the sand his bed.

His tummy starts rumbling
for some bait,
So he lies very still
for a long hard wait.

Along swims a fish
much smaller than him.
There's no hesitation.
Gulp! He gobbles him in.

He's satisfied now
as he looks around.
What a beautiful sight
nowhere else to be found.

The sun glistens on shells
and sparkles on sand.
Fish counts his blessings
he lives on sea . . . not land!

Penny Foster (12)
St John's RC Comprehensive School, Bishop Auckland

HOMEWORK

When school work is done
before the fun
comes homework!
My life is football, computers and TV
but before the fun
comes homework!
My boots are clean, my strip is ready
kick-off draws closer
but before the fun
comes homework!
'Mum, I'll do it later, this match is so important.'
'No!'
The important thing is homework!

Paul Walker (12)
St John's RC Comprehensive School, Bishop Auckland

POETRY

I'm no good at poetry
I don't know what to say
I'll write about anything
As long as it sounds OK!
I then sit at the table
And think of things
Then after a while something rings
I say to myself 'Yes that's all right.
Am I clever or am I just bright?'
Because this poem will be out of sight . . .
Michael Kirtley (12)
St John's RC Comprehensive School, Bishop Auckland

THE BOWLING BALL

My bowling ball is big and round.
It's made of solid wood.
And when it hits the floor
It makes the most almighty sound.
It sounds like a herd of elephants
Jumping in one big thud.

The best part is last of course!
When it hits the pins - it makes them turn and spin.
You hear them go down with a
Bang, clatter, bang!

Every time I go bowling
I take my bowling ball.
With its red shine and round body
It's a killer on the aisle . . .

Philip James Santana Smith (12)
St John's RC Comprehensive School, Bishop Auckland

THE SIMPSON'S FAMILY

I watch the Simpsons on telly
Homer has an enormous belly!
He's got a son called Bart
Who's not at all smart.
Marge is Homer's wife
Who sorts out his miserable life.
Lisa always gets A's on her tests
Her parents think she is the best
Maggie watches The Krusty Show
And hits Homer with a mallet on the toe . . .

Victoria Ratcliffe (12)
St John's RC Comprehensive School, Bishop Auckland

CHRISTMAS

Snow falling on the ground.
Icy wind blowing.
Christmas is not far away
You can tell by the children's faces.
They are excited and cannot sleep
Thinking of the toys and games
That they will soon have
To open on Christmas Day.

They don't seem to care or remember
Whose birthday it is
And why we are celebrating.
It's not just about receiving gifts
But what we should do.
Give peace and goodwill to all.

Robert Jones (12)
St John's RC Comprehensive School, Bishop Auckland

WITCHES' BREW

First for the spell is a stinking smell.
An ear of a rat, a cat and a bat.
Then an eye from a dog
A leg of a frog.
A big slimy snail
A kitten's tail.
A wing of a bird
Once you've stirred
The spell is for who?
It must be for you . . . !
Casey Mangles (12)
St John's RC Comprehensive School, Bishop Auckland

THE CASTLE ON HALLOWEEN

October 31st - the night is here
All my biggest fears surround me.
I look up at the dark silhouette of the castle
as lightning strikes in the distance.
I walk up the pathway,
Crackling, crunching as my feet touch the ground.
The front of the glowing castle appears.
The big wooden strong door in front of us
I reach out for the handle, hands shaking.
Turn the door handle gently
Push the door away from me
I gently walk through the doorway,
My heart beating fast.
My hands tremble as I walk further.
I face the stunning staircase.
The door slams shut behind me
It locks itself
I panic
I try to open it
It's no use
I'm trapped . . .

Michael Hartmann (12)
St John's RC Comprehensive School, Bishop Auckland

THE SEA

We sit on the seashore.
Eyes closed, just to hear
Sound of waves
Splashing, crashing.

We look in the distance
Just to see
A very tall ship
Pounding past me.

A lighthouse on the pier
Flashes light
As rocks close by.
A warning to sailors not to come near.

Darkness falls
The sea calms
Another day ends
Until tomorrow comes.

Gemma Bell (12)
St John's RC Comprehensive School, Bishop Auckland

DOLPHINS
Limbering, leaping dolphins
Diving through the air.
Divine creatures of the sea
Dancing through the air.

Intelligent, lithe dolphins
Darting here and there.
Drifting without a care
Captivating all that see.

Pleasant, smiling dolphins
Gentle as can be.
Cheerful and well-mannered
Gentlemen of the sea.

Dignified, glistening dolphins
Sovereigns of the sea.
Elegant as swans
Magnificent dolphins . . .

Rebecca Ferry (12)
St John's RC Comprehensive School, Bishop Auckland

THE STORM

Still and calm was the sea
Gently rocking the ship.
No clouds to be seen
A perfect day
But not for long . . .

Raging, rolling, pitch-black clouds
Rumbling thunder.
Ferocious crashing lightning illuminated the ocean.
Gale-force winds buffeted the sails
The air turned icy cold.

Tempestuous waves tossed the vessel.
Monsoon-like rain pelted the deck.
Submersion threatened.
Chaos ruled, control was lost.
The ship surrendered to the murky depths.

Gradually the gales diminished
Waves retreated, thunder silenced.
Peace was restored.
Everything was calm.
The ship was no more . . .

Sean Kay (12)
St John's RC Comprehensive School, Bishop Auckland

IT'S TOUGH

It's hard to find
That after all this time
The pain still hasn't left
I think about it all the time.
A bag of dancing images to sift.

Rubbing like a piece of chalk,
My memories turn to dust.
Just
To hold those pictures of you close
Those special moments that we chose
For us . . .

And yet they fall away
Plummeting to sodden ground
And vanishing from sight (existence?)
I touch the lantern so that I might
Search for them
While there is light . . .

And then there I am
Clawing at the earth
To find it comes away in chunks.
Losing myself from the corpreal
My strangled cries the final seal
Nothing left . . .

Where am I
And why am I here?
So far and yet so near.
It's near and then it's
Gone, faded
There is no help for us
Or me . . .

Philip Morris (14)
St Leonard's RC Comprehensive School, Durham City

IT STOOD THERE, GAPING!

I heard a noise in the middle of the night
Tell a lie it was half-past nine.
Was it a ghost or the bogeyman?
Or Dracula waiting to dine?

It stood there, gaping
It was an awful sight.
It was black, or was it blue?
Or maybe it was white!

Never mind what colour it was
It doesn't really matter.
But I feel sure that not before long
Its tummy would be much fatter.

It stood there, gaping.
It was incredibly tall.
Five or six metres, or was that just a shadow?
Creeping up the wall?

Never mind how tall it was
It doesn't really matter.
But I felt sure that not before long
Its tummy would be much fatter.

Now just calm down,
Let me see!
Come in, kind sir
Fancy some tea?

The window rattled
On the windowpane.
The rain it poured and the thunder it roared
As the bus drove up the lane.

All of a sudden it walked to the door.
Reached out and turned on the light,
And then I saw the monstrosity
That had given me such a fright

I had heard a noise in the middle of the night
Though I think it was twenty to ten.
It wasn't a ghost or a bogeyman
It was only my brother . . . Ben!

Jessica Myles (13)
St Leonard's RC Comprehensive School, Durham City

THE TEACHER FROM HEAVEN/THE TEACHER FROM HELL

What's a teacher from heaven?
A teacher that lets you go on the bell.
What's a teacher from heaven?
A teacher who's kind and forgiving.
What's a teacher from heaven?
A teacher that praises you.
What's a teacher from heaven?
A teacher that's explaining and understanding.

What's a teacher from hell?
A teacher that's racist.
What's a teacher from hell?
A teacher that's full of anger.
What's a teacher from hell?
A teacher that's slow and boring.
What's a teacher from hell?
A teacher that always shouts at you.

Scott Kimmins (13)
St Leonard's RC Comprehensive School, Durham City

A POEM ABOUT ANGER
WHO COULD IT BE?
Who could it be?
The person who has taken my make-up, money and CDs.
Who could it be?
Man or woman, rich or poor.
Who could it be?
My own family, or even one of my friends.
Who could it be?
The anger is boiling inside me, this is not funny anymore.
Who could it be?
The person must be dishonest, but the question still remains
Who could it be?
My things have returned, out of the blue.
Who could it be?
I've just found out, and there's no doubt
Who could it be?
A small boy of five has rifled through my room and taken my things.
Who could it be?
My little brother Jonathan, the angel with black wings.

Ruth Elder (13)
St Leonard's RC Comprehensive School, Durham City

AUTUMN
Now is the time for days to grow shorter.
Cold breezes blow the leaves from the trees.
The earth is closing down for its winter rest.
All around are the glorious colours of autumn.
We are surrounded by the richness of the colours.
Autumn is a lovely season - misty, colourful and bright.

Emma Scales (13)
St Leonard's RC Comprehensive School, Durham City

IS THERE ANY NEED?

A netball match,
A non-contact game.
So why the need to push and shove!
Is there really any need?

A scratch on the arm,
Then elbowing and punching.
She's trying to push me off-side,
But I've done nothing to deserve this.
Is there really any need?

I've got the ball,
Now I can score.
But *she's* there again,
With her arms in my face,
Fouling for sure.
Is there any need?
Is there really any need?

Her piercing green eyes
Staring at me.
Her hands outstretched
Preventing the ball from reaching the net.
Is there really any need?

I've got to get my own back,
A push here and there.
I want to show this green-eyed monster that I'm not afraid,
And wipe that smug smile right off her face.
Is there any need?
Is there really any need?
Yes! There definitely is a need!

Katherine Hannah (13)
St Leonard's RC Comprehensive School, Durham City

MY ANGER STRIKES

What was that remark?
What did you say?
Getting frustrated
Burning up
Reaching my boiling point
Up and up.
I'm going to explode
Clenching my hands
Tighter and tighter.
My nails digging into my palms
As I stamp my feet up the stairs.
Trying to absorb the shock of my feet hitting the ground.
Then through my bedroom door
Using every muscle in my body,
To slam it behind me.
The noise of my teeth, grinding together
Trying to crush my teeth.
Making as much noise as possible.
I thought of the sarcastic remark,
And counted to ten.
I relaxed, and my anger had past
Who knows when my anger will strike again . . .

Joy Hewitson (14)
St Leonard's RC Comprehensive School, Durham City

QUESTIONS

Why is the sky blue?
Why is the grass green?
Why do cows say moo?
And why is the queen well . . . queen?

Why do I have to eat my tea?
Why are daisies white?
Why am I me?
And why do some animals bite?

Ruth Wilson (11)
St Leonard's RC Comprehensive School, Durham City

ANGER VS PAIN!

'Come here!'
Aaahh . . .
Like a bowling ball hitting a strike between my legs
From her foot . . .
Falling to the ground, like a leaf in autumn.
Wanting to get up, trying to get up.
Wanting to shout, trying, trying
Pain over coming anger.
Blackness before my eyes
As pain shoots through me like a bullet.
Writhing on the floor in pain.
With difficulty, I stand up
I shout, I scream at her!

Again the foot . . .
Like a thunderbolt from Thor.
Again the pain . . .
Felled once again, like a tree in the forest.
I shout, I scream at her!

Neil Thomas (14)
St Leonard's RC Comprehensive School, Durham City

THE TEACHER FROM HELL

The teacher from hell is ugly and fat
He sits on his desk
Looking over his tall hat
He sits there not moving a limb
Oh my God, he's really dim
I see him in the hall with his detention slips
I stand there shaking from fingers to tips
He's coming closer, I'm in his sight
He says 'What are those on your feet?'
I answer 'Trainers Sir'
He tells me to sit in the dreaded seat
I take of my trainers, put on my shoes
I stood up and ran
Like I have nothing to lose.

Danielle Horn (13)
St Leonard's RC Comprehensive School, Durham City

WHEN I WAS ANNOYED

The shelves were full, *smash!*
The things had come off it, *smash!*
My fists had struck the objects, *smash!*
The CDs were next, *smash!*
My fist cut through them, like a knife through butter, *smash!*
His bedroom was ablaze with destruction, *smash!*
My brother will not forget that, *smash!*
Ben Coates (13)
St Leonard's RC Comprehensive School, Durham City

ANGER

Storm upstairs, slam door,
anger boils up.
Balls hit cupboards,
fists hit walls,
anger boils up.
Fall asleep - in a mood,
wake up, storm around,
'I'm in a mood!'
Anger boils up,
anger explodes,
break down,
sorry Mam,
I was wrong.
Anger cools down,
bed early tomorrow.

Paul Greensitt (13)
St Leonard's RC Comprehensive School, Durham City

A MOMENT OF MADNESS

The calm, peaceful morning air
Is shattered by a piercing cry.
A white-hot poker jabs my arm
I feel hot pain then overwhelming anger,
Rage igniting in my head,
Through blood-red vision I wield a stick.
A raging fire burns within me,
Scorching anger drives me on.
Swipe! Swipe! Revenge is sweet.
Satisfaction quells anger once more.
A dead, crippled wasp - lying at my feet . . .

Andrew Lacey (13)
St Leonard's RC Comprehensive School, Durham City

I HAD A DREAM

I scored a goal in last night's dream,
I was the hero of the winning team.
The England captain knew I could score,
And when I did, all I heard was the roar.

I sprinted hard up the field,
Not thinking that this could be real.
Between two defenders appeared a gap,
So I gave the ball an almighty whack.

The keeper stood with such surprise,
How could a situation like this arise?
I imagined the gleams of the winning Cup,
Could this just be my good luck?

Bang! It went in, the crowd went mad,
I was then extremely glad.
I was the finest player on my team,
Well! That's the way that it seemed.

'Come on get up!' I heard my mum say,
What a way to start the day.
Was that goal really true?
Or was I the only one who ever knew?

Sarah Williams (13)
St Leonard's RC Comprehensive School, Durham City

BUT YOU SAID NEXT WEEK!

'You can spend it next week,'
The words hung in my ears.
'You can spend it next week,'
A slight grin appears.

I can buy what I need,
I've got my own money.
Whatever I want,
It is all my money.

I could buy a fast car,
Or even a boat.
I could buy a big tank,
Or castle and moat.

We are going today,
All my thinking's been done.
We are going today,
I'm going with my mum.

But Mum comes and tells me,
'There's just not enough time.'
My eyes fill with anger,
That anger of mine.

'But you said next week!'
I storm up the stairs,
I slam all the doors,
'It's just not fair!'

Adam Sinclair (13)
St Leonard's RC Comprehensive School, Durham City

THE CAT

The light tore into my sticky eyes.
An alarm clock-bearing messenger,
Sits waiting for me to awaken,
Ring ring, ring ring.
Her metallic, ringing, soft miaows,
Were gunshots in my ears.
Begrudgingly I let her out,
Ring ring, ring ring.
The calm was torn by claws on wood,
Light awoke the room again,
No mercy, my target was surely locked,
Ring ring, ring ring.
She happily sat with ignorance,
Until the dodge, the run, the jump,
I pushed her to the floor,
Ring ring, ring ring.
The weight was taken off my head,
The fire put out inside,
Tiredness swept my bloodshot eyes,
Ring ring, rim rmmm . . .

Matthew Adamson (14)
St Leonard's RC Comprehensive School, Durham City

HELL POEM

There it was the old school bell
And ringing it was the teacher from hell.
I felt like I was sitting in some old prison cell.
'Have you done your homework?' she would scream and yell.
I would think to myself 'Dear Lord, just let us out of this hell.'

Karen Davies (13)
St Leonard's RC Comprehensive School, Durham City

FRUSTRATION!

Urgent phone call, ignorant brother,
Good combination?
I don't think so, *frustration!*
'Please get off the phone,' I called.
'Get off the phone Stephen,' I shouted.
'Now!' I screamed.
He refused, simply refused to respond,
Frustration!
Then miraculously he hung up,
I dived for the phone but . . .
That very second in an annoying manner,
The phone rang and,
Guess what?
It was for Stephen.

Ellena Plumb (13)
St Leonard's RC Comprehensive School, Durham City

SORRY MUM

When I was younger, about seven or eight,
I wanted to stay up and watch telly till late.
My mum said 'No,' I needed my sleep,
So I went upstairs and got up to mischief.
A lovely gold ring that my mum bought for me,
I twisted and chewed and then smiled with glee.
I'll show her, or so I thought,
But the tables turned when I was caught.
My mum was sad, it was plain to see,
I'm really sorry I got so angry.
Katy Moore (14)
St Leonard's RC Comprehensive School, Durham City

LOST IT!

Irritating cousins,
Shut up!
Annoying brother,
Shut up!
How dare they?
Their cheek, ignorance.
Ignore them,
Must finish essays,
Must complete work,
Shut up!
Go to sleep!
Temper rising,
Lost it!

Anna Wigham (16)
St Leonard's RC Comprehensive School, Durham City

TWO OF US

My friend and I
Arranged - promised
The 2 of us
Together
2 tickets
2 friends
1 choice
2 of us
To just me
Betrayed.

Katharine Dent (16)
St Leonard's RC Comprehensive School, Durham City

HERE'S THE TWIST

Holiday
Go-kart racing
Green light
Go!
Accelerating
Out in front
Overtaking
Suddenly,
Red light flashing!
Accident!
Other car skidding
Slam on brake
Slow down
Stop!
Boy not slowing down
My car in way
Look out!
Bang!
Pain
My car sliding
Boy laughing
Anger rising
Get out
Shouting
Boy apologising
Me complaining
Here's the twist
The *little* boy was too
Small for the ride.

Jamie Heels (16)
St Leonard's RC Comprehensive School, Durham City

A NIGHT OUT
Paranoid,
Eyes watching,
Glaring,
Staring,
Sat upon you,
Paranoid,
Hot and sweaty,
Music pumping,
Bodies squashed,
All together,
Lights are blazing,
Humid, dingy,
Bodies together,
One by one,
Feel out of place,
Where to turn,
Eyes watching,
Glaring,
Staring,
Eyes watching,
Paranoid.

Nicola Heron (16)
St Leonard's RC Comprehensive School, Durham City

I LIKE, I DON'T
I like sunny days,
Rainy days I don't.
I like reading,
Writing I won't.

I like chocolate,
I like sweets.
I like history,
And I love to eat.

I love football,
I don't like ice hockey.
I like music,
And I don't like coffee.

I like science,
I like maths.
I like English,
And most of all I like learning about the past.

Stephanie Ann Brain (11)
St Leonard's RC Comprehensive School, Durham City

SNAKES
S nakes in the grass,
S lithering quite fast,
N o scent, no sound,
A lthough knowing what's around.
K idney feast of
E very beast.
S cent-catching tongues,
S uper-fanged, with great lungs.

S lithering quietly,
L iving highly.
I n sheltered place, in
T heir own pace.
H oping for the best,
E nding their time of no rest.
R eeling or snarling
I n danger of falling from
N ow to then,
G rown to hate men.

Peter David Langridge (12)
St Leonard's RC Comprehensive School, Durham City

THE HIDDEN SIDE

Like the melting of wax,
she makes the hardest of people soft,
And the most closed personalities open,
like a dandelion in sunlight.

She moves with lightning strike
to, and from her victims.
She doesn't judge. Is unconditional,
supposedly everlasting?

People rarely see her other side.
The side that makes people cheat,
the side that is unfair, and
causes conflict.

Like the cooling of wax,
she makes the softest personalities hard,
and like a dandelion at night,
she makes the most open personalities close.

This side makes people unstable.
This side makes people hate.
This side makes people cry.

She's easy to fall out of.
Carol Reid (16)
St Leonard's RC Comprehensive School, Durham City

SHARK

A famous predator of the sea,
Gliding through the water, like a bird from the sky,
Hunting its prey with razor-sharp teeth,
The shark, what an amazing animal!

Recognised by humans as such a deadly creature,
But through the eyes of a shark,
It is such a silly thing to say,
For the shark,
While powerful and strong in every way,
Is just another animal,
With not a single bad intention.

Its rough sandpaper skin,
Brushing against the current,
Its long pointy snout,
Guiding it on its way,
The ragged, razor teeth,
Used to tear apart and rip,
The sensitive nostrils,
Which sensor many things.

The shark is not as fierce,
As many people think,
It is just a graceful hunter,
Of the darkest, darkest deep.

Louise Watson (11)
St Leonard's RC Comprehensive School, Durham City

AN ANIMAL POEM

The best animal in the world is the tiger, he rules the jungle.
He is so strong, if he looks at you, you get frightened,
So you must not disturb him,
Otherwise he can tear you into pieces.
He can run at 100 miles an hour.
He is the best.
I love him.
I just wish I was him,
Because he is so strong and fast.
I could just beat every runner in the world.
He can be rather dangerous,
With his claws as sharp as knives.
His teeth are like a chainsaw,
So if you don't do anything to them,
They will do nothing to you.
I wish I could go to Africa on a safari,
To watch all the tigers run like mad.
The best thing I like about tigers is when they chase their prey,
But I think I will never go to Africa.

Luis Enrique Ojeda-Garay (11)
St Leonard's RC Comprehensive School, Durham City

AN UNFAITHFUL SLEEP

You drifted away
And watched me sleep,
As the dreamers dreamed,
And the keeper keeps
Me gently in her warm embrace,
For I won't drown
In her shallow face.
No, I can't drown
In this unreal place.

I slept forever,
And timely dreamed
That you had severed
My only means
To hold you in my deceived embrace,
For I won't die
In her guilty face,
I would live a lie
Just to suit her taste.

Peter J Earnshaw (16)
St Leonard's RC Comprehensive School, Durham City

TIGERS

Tigers are big cats
They live in the wild
They're not like pussy cats
Who live as pets
Tigers scare people, but not me!

Tigers are striped
They're orange and black
They hunt for their food
They're usually big
Tigers scare people, but not me!

Tigers roar loudly
They don't miaow
They run fast
They live in the jungle
Tigers scare people, but not me!

Mark Herkes (11)
St Leonard's RC Comprehensive School, Durham City

ANTICIPATING A DREAM?

A vivid memory of anxiety,
Waiting for an influential piece of paper.
Grades.
My parents hoping, expecting and eager.
Grades.
A brown envelope conceals my worth.
Grades.
Without hesitation I stare at its contents.
Anxiety, grades.
Success spells out my aspirations.
Grades.
Ecstasy!

Anna Wass (16)
St Leonard's RC Comprehensive School, Durham City

THE TEACHER FROM HELL!

Aghhh, the teacher from hell.
She never lets us out on the bell.
She's always so rotten.
If homework's forgotten.
And she will have your head.
Aghhh, the teacher from hell.
Her nose . . .
There's a tale to tell.
It's so long and hooked.
Look twice and you're booked.
That is our teacher from hell.

Kameron Kafai (13)
St Leonard's RC Comprehensive School, Durham City

AN ANIMAL POEM
I look like a lion
Thumping through the night,
I smell of green leaves and grass.
The best animal is the lion.
I roar through the night looking for a fight,
I sound like a herd of wildebeests.
My teeth are like sharp knives,
My mane is very long.
I do not make a sound.
I'm getting hot,
The sun is shining bright.
I move very slowly
Through the long grass
waiting.
Joseph O'Keeffe (11)
St Leonard's RC Comprehensive School, Durham City

TWO SIDES
Surface, is kind.
Change of state,
Hostile intention,
Selfishness, wearing.
I can see - but is it
Just me?
Hatred I *must* conceal
For, this evil only I can see.
Evil - how bad, can it be?

Victoria Judd (17)
St Leonard's RC Comprehensive School, Durham City

TEACHER FROM HELL

Dishing out report cards here and there,
When it comes to homework, I wish he didn't care,
With kindness out the window, and patience, that's a joke!
I wish we had an interest in any word he spoke,
Here are some words to describe this nasty bloke:
Ugly,
Harmful,
Spiteful,
Horrid,
Unpleasant,
And offensive.
And he never lets us out before the bell,
That just about sums up my teacher from hell.

Andrew Corrigan (13)
St Leonard's RC Comprehensive School, Durham City

MY BEDROOM

Mother said 'Go tidy your room, here's a duster,
Polish and a broom.'
I went upstairs with a heavy heart,
I didn't know quite where to start.
I opened the door and looked with shame,
I alone was to blame.
Cups, saucers, bowls and plates,
Tennis rackets, roller skates.
Everything just lying there,
I turned to leave in despair.
My mother shouted 'Get it done.'
Being a slob is no fun.

Joseph Martin (11)
St Leonard's RC Comprehensive School, Durham City

GOLD

Hands on, are you ready? Lift
Here goes
Good luck
Focus
Race your own race
Focus

Race 124, on the start please
Concentrate
Attention, go!

500 meters gone
Pain
Well done
Help

500 to go
No, not 3rd!
Well done
Pain
Take it home
Joint 2nd!
Now we're moving
We're ahead!
10 strokes .
Amazing
Gold
Smiles, shouts, screams, hurting, hugs, honour.
Awake.
Catherine Cantwell (16)
St Leonard's RC Comprehensive School, Durham City

159

THE TEACHER FROM HEAVEN AND HELL

The teacher from heaven:
What is a teacher from heaven?
Kind and caring.
What is a teacher from heaven?
Someone who has a nice voice.
What is a teacher from heaven?
Someone who treats people the same.
What is a teacher from heaven?
A teacher who is very understanding.
What is a teacher from heaven?
Someone who is very funny.

The teacher from hell:
T   ells you off all the time,
E   very lesson work, work, work,
A   ll the time not satisfied,
C   alling you out to read all the time,
H   er voice is so annoying,
E   ach day the same,
R   eally boring.

F   irmly she convicts,
R   elentlessly she convicts,
•   n time we have to hand in homework,
M   ore often than not she gives us detention.
H   er good lesson is an hour of writing,
E   arly we arrive,
L   ate we leave,
L   essons are so boring with *the teacher from hell.*

Aidan Keith (13)
St Leonard's RC Comprehensive School, Durham City

PANTHER

I have a mini panther sitting on my bed,
It's not pink or blue or even red.
It's black with claws as sharp as nails,
Its colour is fierce, not dull or pale.
The mini panther is a hunter, he prowls among the trees,
A mouse is the target, he's getting very keen.
He waits and waits then pounces at the timid mouse,
With the small rodent in his mouth, he makes his way to his house.
He comes in and sits on my knee,
He is very tired after prowling in the trees.
I stroke him and he falls asleep,
Then suddenly up he leaps.
He sees a moving target running across the floor,
He walks so quietly then belts behind the door.
Five minutes later he walks back in the house,
He's caught another field mouse.
He sits by the fire and eats his mouse on his mat,
I love him because he's my black cat.

Luke Foster (12)
St Leonard's RC Comprehensive School, Durham City

WHEREVER I GO

Wherever I go
Whatever I do
Going to the park
Even going out with you
Whenever I see you my heart melts
You have got the looks
You're in my books
So when we are together
It will be so much better.

Nicola Slee (13)
St Leonard's RC Comprehensive School, Durham City

THE MAGICAL WORLD OF READING

When I read,
I escape into a magical world . . .
Instead of pages of words,
I see visions and scenes.
Whenever I turn a page,
I wonder what awaits,
Death, sorrow, pain or
Life, joy and celebration.
I dread the end of a book:-
You never know what type of ending is lurking,
Hiding in the last chapter.
I always find reading a thrill,
Try it and see how much fun books can be!

Francesca Mastaglio (11)
St Leonard's RC Comprehensive School, Durham City

SALLY

My uncle's got this dog called Sally,
She's great fun but a bit doolally.
Me and my brother were playing with a ball,
Sally went after it and jumped over a wall.
After a hard day's work I went to bed,
Sally jumped on it to rest her head.
The next day I was in the river having a play,
Sally jumped in, I couldn't get out of the way.
I was soaked, drenched right through,
But Sally I still think you're a great dog too.

Gregory Piskosz (11)
St Leonard's RC Comprehensive School, Durham City

A POEM ABOUT COMPUTERS

Computers are good for work and play,
Look on the web sites (co. UK).
You can go on the Internet with a modem,
Hack into databases and cause mayhem.
Sometimes it will crash if it is broken,
You type with your fingers, words are not spoken.
Puzzles and games can be really fun,
When you turn on your computer the fun's just begun.
I think computers can be really great,
But when they're not working it fills me with hate.
You can use computers for all sorts of things,
Memorising data or sending messages to kings.

Oliver Burke (12)
St Leonard's RC Comprehensive School, Durham City

CRUELTY TO ANIMALS

Cruelty to animals, this makes me sad
neglect, hunger, pain
it drives me mad.
Frightened, cold, shivering with fear
sad little eyes
I'm full of tears.
Prosecute the cruel owners
send them to jail
let them shiver and suffer
it's their turn to wail.

Rachel Higgin (11)
St Leonard's RC Comprehensive School, Durham City

MY FAVOURITE ANIMAL

There are chickens, there are frogs,
I like cats, and I like dogs.
Fish can swim,
Cows can roam,
Though hamsters are small
And elephants are big,
My favourite animal, has to be a
Pig!

There are rabbits, there are mice,
I like guinea pigs, yeah, they're nice.
Birds can fly,
Snakes can slither,
Though hamsters are small
And elephants are big,
My favourite animal, has to be a
Pig!

Emily Ashfield (11)
St Leonard's RC Comprehensive School, Durham City

THE WIND IS BLOWING

The wind is blowing outside my house
The leaves are leaping all around
The days are flying by
The leaves are no exception
All the people stop and stare as the leaves spell out my name
I look at all their faces
They're all as white as snow
As if they saw a ghost.

Joseph Waggott (12)
St Leonard's RC Comprehensive School, Durham City

HOMEWORK

Homework, homework, it's such a bore,
The teacher says 'It will help you so much more.'
Tonight we want to go out and play,
So please don't give us any today.

Oh no! He's going to win,
'Take out your planners,' he says with a grin.
There's no way of stopping him,
The whole class looks grim.

From the back of the room there's a groan,
He looks up and says 'Did I hear a moan?
For that I'll give you ten more times I think,'
I'd rather be washing up at the kitchen sink.

Homework, homework, it's such a bore,
The teacher says 'It will help you so much more.'
Tonight we want to go out and play,
So please don't give us any more today.

Vicki Taylorson (11)
St Leonard's RC Comprehensive School, Durham City

ZAK SCOTT

Z ak Scott is my name,
A nd playing football is my aim.
K icking a football is what I do,

S ometimes I might have a game with you.
C ycling I also like,
•   n my little brother's bike.
T o the shop and around about,
T hen I get home and I really shout.

Zak Scott (12)
St Leonard's RC Comprehensive School, Durham City

My Dog

I hear her little paws pitter-patter across the ground
I see her little round mouth greeting me with a growling sound
I feel her warm pink tongue brushing against my face
I watch her trot along with all her pride and grace

I hear her pleading cry asking me to play
I see her sparkling eyes, they look so merry and gay
I feel her soft brown fur brush against my legs
I watch her spring from place to place with happiness in her head

I hear her softly sigh as she wanders to her bed
I see her gently lie and rest her tiny head
I feel her warm round body as she settles down to sleep
I watch her wriggle gently as she counts those endless sheep.

Fiona Durbridge (11)
St Leonard's RC Comprehensive School, Durham City

My Poem About A Mole

Deep, deep down in mud and the dirt where the long mole hides,
He fancies slugs and bugs for his dinner time.
Yesterday's washing off the line,
And upon the mole's bed it lies.
Snug as a bug as he lies in his mud,
For a cosy day inside
With his bugs and his slugs for his dinner time.
'Wiggly bugs and slugs are very tasty indeed,' he says,
Because they're made for a mole in his hole at dinner time.

Nicola Scott (11)
St Leonard's RC Comprehensive School, Durham City

GIANT SQUID

Giant squid, or so it is said,
Live at the bottom of the seabed.
This great and powerful beast,
Will gorge, guzzle, feed and feast,
On whatever happens to float by,
Even if it is the size of a fly!

Usually it has dark skin at sight,
It changes illuminous at a fright.
With one massive beady eye,
Any movement it will spy.
With eight tentacles it is scary,
Like a spider, but not hairy!

Up to 100 metres in length,
Need I say more about his strength?
No one really knows his noise,
You can't tell 1000s of metres under sea buoys.
Sucking in water and pushing it back out,
Is his way of stealthily moving about.

Sperm whales are who they fight,
In the darkness of seabed night.
They are the only ones who really know,
Anything about their deadly foe.
Even with the technology today,
We can do nothing except keep the excitement at bay!

Robert Jones (11)
St Leonard's RC Comprehensive School, Durham City

MY PIGGY WIGGY
I used to have a pink fat pig
With a curly-wurly tail
Sticking-out ears
And a bow on top of her head

I used to have a pink fat pig
With a curly-wurly tail
I bought this piggy wiggy
In a jumble sale

She sang, read
And danced for me
And cooked and baked cakes
That's why she was my special piggy wiggy

She gardened, cleaned
And ironed and brushed my hair
She did everything that I asked
Then I decided she had to be my favourite piggy wiggy

She won races, competitions
And toys for me
Every day I got fond of her
Then she became the world's best piggy wiggy

Then one day a Chinaman came
And butchered her
As any old pig
Now I don't have a piggy wiggy.

Hei Won Ahn (11)
St Leonard's RC Comprehensive School, Durham City

ANGER

Tracksuit bottoms,
Who needs them?
Tracksuit bottoms,
Who cares?
Can't find any I like,
But can't leave without a pair.

Stupid sales assistant,
Who needs them?
Pushing clothes down my throat,
Who cares?
Don't want to buy anything at all,
As he shows me another skirt I won't wear.

I can feel my dragon approaching,
I can feel its fiery breath,
Then I blow up in flames and attack them,
With my sharp claws I rip them to shreds.

People turn to look at me,
As I burn things to the ground.
I stare at their ignorant faces,
As my acid tongue spits a poisoned sound.

Tempers, I say,
Who needs them?
People back away,
Who cares?
Then I open my wings to the sky,
And fly off into the air!

Kathryn Mason (13)
St Leonard's RC Comprehensive School, Durham City

I SAW A BLACK COLT!

(Dedicated to Millish, my lovely black colt)
I saw a black colt one day,
up by a fence swaying from left to right.
His ears were pricked,
he gave a gentle nudge
and a sweet little whinny.
His mother was standing close
keeping an eye on him while grazing.
She gave a loud *neigh*
and he trotted to her and
grazed by her side.
A lovely black colt!
Kayleigh Wilkinson (11)
St Leonard's RC Comprehensive School, Durham City